Behavioral

Objective

Sequence

Sheldon Braaten

Research Press
2612 North Mattis Avenue
Champaign, Illinois 61822
(800) 519-2707   www.researchpress.com

Composition & cover design by Suzanne Wagner
Printed by Total Printing Systems

ISBN-13: 978-0-87822-384-8
ISBN-10: 0-87822-384-3

Library of Congress Control Number 98-68262

Contents

Acknowledgments

The first draft of the *Behavioral Objective Sequence* (BOS) was completed in 1976 with contributions from the special education staff of the Minneapolis Public Schools' special school program for adolescents with serious emotional and behavioral disorders. Over the next ten years of development, numerous revisions were made leading to its adoption for use in a variety of special education programs serving students ranging in age from kindergarten through high school. Beginning in 1990, a series of statistical studies was conducted to establish the reliability and validity attributes of the BOS and to suggest further changes for refinement. I wish to express a sincere thanks to the many people whose comments and participation in developmental activities have contributed much to this edition of the BOS. A particular "thank you" is extended to Dr. Frank H. Wood, Professor Emeritus, University of Minnesota, for his endless encouragement, thoughtful comments, and contributions to the section on functional analysis for intervention planning. A special acknowledgment and note of appreciation is for Dr. Mary M. Wood, Professor Emeritus, University of Georgia, for providing to our field the "Developmental Therapy" model, which has been the inspiration for the organizational framework of the BOS.

Introduction

Of the many and varying challenges presented by students with disabilities, those related to providing appropriate services to children and youth with serious emotional and behavioral disorders (EBD) are among the most difficult for educators and other service providers. A key to success, and the cornerstone of contemporary practice, is the delivery of individualized services and the development of intervention plans that are based on a thorough assessment of students' existing strengths and needs or deficits. Meeting the complex needs of these students is contingent upon, and defined by, procedures for identifying realistic goals and specific behavioral objectives and a carefully orchestrated set of interventions implemented over a sustained period of time. While the determination of needed services is linked to identified long-term goals, the daily activities of direct-service providers are, of necessity, more focused on the achievement of specific behavioral objectives.

The *Behavioral Objective Sequence* (BOS) was constructed to assist special educators and other professionals assess behavioral competencies of students with EBD and to determine developmentally appropriate objectives, from which detailed intervention plans can be prepared. The BOS initially was used with students referred for placement and/or being served in special classes or special school settings. However, throughout the history of its use, practitioners in various roles have found the BOS useful and adaptable to a variety of other settings, including those for students presenting other primary disabilities, but who also exhibit challenging behavior.

The BOS Construction

The general organization and construction of the BOS is a scope and sequence of behavioral objectives (skills) that are essential to the success of children and youth in social and school contexts. It represents an integration of behavioral and developmental concepts, and in particular, the influence of M. M. Wood's model of "Developmental Therapy" (Wood, 1981; Wood, Davis, Swindle, & Quirk, 1996). The BOS consists of 233 items arranged in six subscales:

1. Adaptive Behaviors
2. Self-Management Behaviors
3. Communication Behaviors
4. Interpersonal Behaviors
5. Task Behaviors
6. Personal Behaviors

Each subscale is a domain of related and sequenced skills derived from task analysis, deductive logic, and child and adolescent development literature. Each of the subscales also contains within it several related "sub-subscales" of hierarchically arranged goals and objectives across three levels. Each of the three levels designates an *a priori* determined dividing line between skills that are associated with developmental age ranges or levels. Level 3 skills (the 300-level goals and objectives) are basic skills typically mastered by very young children (before grade 1) without disabilities. Level 2 skills (the 200-level goals and objectives) are generally mastered by children during the elementary school years. Level 1 skills (the 100-level goals and objectives) are typically achieved by adolescents and young adults. Within each level, the BOS construction includes different and increasingly more developmentally complex goals and objectives.*

* *Note:* There is no specific reason other than the author's choice for the use of 3-2-1 vs. 1-2-3. Historically, levels of service models have referred to least intensive services with the lowest number and more intensive services with higher numbers, e.g., level 1 = regular class and level 6 = residential.

The BOS is not intended to be an exhaustive list of behavioral objectives, but it does include items that address the range and breadth of skills acquired throughout children's development from early childhood through adolescence, and particularly those that are essential to success in a school setting. It does not include academic content objectives. It does include work readiness behaviors and transition skills, but not objectives related to specific career or vocational areas. The BOS is not a psychological test or measure of personality. It is based on the assumption that while individuals do develop in similar and predictable basic patterns, there is also great variance among individuals. It should not be assumed that all students will progress or master the skills within the BOS in a similar manner.

The BOS is broad enough to address most planning needs for students with difficult behavior, yet succinct enough for use in preparing an Individual Education Plan (IEP) or an Individual Treatment Plan (ITP). A comprehensive assessment process will include data from a variety of instruments, including the BOS, and provide the information needed to readily determine which objectives are, and are not, mastered by the student. This determination will provide the relevant goals and objectives for an IEP/ITP, along with direct implications for the development of specific intervention plans for each identified objective.

Procedures for Selecting Goals and Objectives

The evaluation of behavioral skills–strengths and deficits–can be a complex, multidimensional task. Further, the selection and use of appropriate measures to identify students as EBD is a serious matter. Such a label can result in negative personal and social consequences for children and youth. Thus, evaluators must take care to be certain that assessment conclusions are based on the highest level of professional standards. The BOS, like any other tool, should be used with full consideration of the essential purpose of an evaluation, which is to know the student, not to label the student.

The BOS has been written, and is intended, to be read literally with a minimum of interpretation. The objectives are, to the extent possible, descriptions of observable behaviors. They are not intended to be associated with gender, culture, or other defined subgroups. Specific examples are provided for each objective to add clarity.

Before completing a BOS evaluation, the user is strongly advised to read through the entire document to gain a knowledge of all the items included and how they are organized. Experienced users will note that only after several readings will one be fully aware of all the items and their relationships within and across subscales. Given the significant variance that exists within and among students with EBD, it is both difficult and important to determine valid and individually relevant objectives. The BOS can be used in three different ways: as a bank of objectives, as a rating scale, or as a structured observation system.

Using the BOS as a Bank of Objectives

The BOS may simply be used as a menu, or bank of goals and objectives, from which evaluators can select relevant items to use in the development of an IEP/ITP. This approach is dependent upon the gathering and review of assessment data from various other sources such as informal observations, interviews, other rating scales, standardized instruments, and professional judgments. The most simple, but also least accurate, procedure is to make a "professional judgment" about whether or not a student has mastered an objective. A better procedure is to have a team of people make a consensus judgment that is based on a careful review of multiple data sources.

Using the BOS as a Rating Scale

The BOS includes a Rating Scale Guide and Current Performance Form that can be used to establish the student's current level of performance on the objectives (see the Appendix). The Rating Scale Guide is a four-point, rate-based scale that indicates the frequency that an objective is performed by the student, ranging from never or rarely to always or almost always. The rate-based approach does not require inferences about "internal states" or assumptions about what one *can do*. Rather, it is focused on what one does do. A rating should be completed only by individuals who have had direct experience with the student over an extended period of time. Administration of a rating scale represents the rater's perception at a moment in time and evaluators should note that these ratings are vulnerable to a variety of "observer biases." These bias effects can be diminished by use of multiple ratings, multiple raters, and by team consensus ratings.

Using the BOS as a Structured Observation System

The third and most accurate approach is to use structured direct observation procedures. The BOS includes Baseline Recording Forms and a Daily Monitoring Record (see the Appendix). Structured observation requires considerable skill, time, and adherence to established protocols. Current levels of performance are established by obtaining baseline rates on the BOS items over an interval that may take up to 2 weeks.

Establishing Mastery Criteria

Each approach will require the user to first establish a criterion for defining mastery (e.g., 80% or 90%) for a fixed interval of time (e.g., 5, 6, or 10 weeks). Procedures for determining mastery criteria may vary depending upon the philosophy or orientation of the evaluator, the purpose for using the BOS, or the extent of knowledge one has about the student. Typically, it is wise to set high mastery standards (e.g., 80%-90% of opportunities over intervals of not less than 5 or 6 weeks). Troubled and troubling students present problem behaviors that have developed and persisted over a long period of time. Thus, these behaviors may be viewed as similar to habits that are often very resistant to change. Replacing established patterns of behavior with new skills generally requires intervention over sustained intervals with many opportunities for the new skills to be practiced and reinforced.

More frequent recordings or observations provide evaluators with increased confidence in the accuracy of their determinations. However, since the structured observation methods are both very time consuming and difficult, and in some situations not possible, methods that include time samples or ratings by multiple team members can be the most useful. Ideally, the system to select objectives will be subsequently useful for monitoring progress on the identified objectives.

Using the BOS Current Performance Form

After a baseline recording procedure has been chosen, record the assessment outcomes on the Current Performance Form, which lists all of the 233 objectives in abbreviated form (see the Appendix). The objectives are numbered with a 3-digit numbering system. The first digit (3, 2, or 1) represents the level of the objectives, and the second and third digits are the numerical sequence of objectives, ranging from 01 to 49. This 3-digit numbering system allows the user two options.

The first option is to simply use the BOS as a numerical sequence of items. The second option is to use the first digit to determine the current level of performance (highest items mastered) as an indicator of a student's developmental level of social functioning. As discussed previously in the section on the BOS construction, the 300-level objectives are those typically mastered by very young children (before grade 1) without disabilities, the 200-level objectives are those typically mastered by children during the elementary school years, and the 100-level objectives are those typically mastered by adolescents and young adults.

This division of levels should not be used as a fixed criterion for age- or grade-related decisions, but it can be helpful for establishing general structures and procedures for services within a program or to differentiate structures between programs based on the characteristics or skill levels of the student(s). The performance levels can also be used to establish criteria for movement, transition, or promotion within a program or to a different option on the continuum of services.

Using the BOS for Identifying Objectives and Long-Term Goals

On the Current Performance Form, begin with the first item in the Adaptive subscale (301) and in the space provided, mark a "√ " to indicate that the objective is mastered or "X" if it is not. If you have no basis for marking a specific objective, insert the abbreviation for "Not Observed" (NO) or "Does Not Apply" (NA). Proceed down the column until every item has been marked. Complete the remaining five subscales. If you are using the rating scale method (see page 5), insert the number (1-4) which most accurately represents the student's current performance; record 0 if you have no basis for judgment or if the objective does not apply in your setting. Long-term goals related to the selected objectives are included at each level within the six subscales.

This method may result in the identification of many skills to be achieved over time. For intervention planning, and as a practical matter, the identified objectives beyond the initial few in each subscale should be viewed as skills to be achieved upon mastery of the earliest objectives selected. In some cases, it also may be very appropriate to consider later objectives as long-term goals themselves.

Using the BOS for Identifying Short-Term Objectives

The short-term, or ceiling, method follows the procedures described above; however, you proceed until you have identified four objectives in each subscale that are *not* mastered and then stop. The objectives that are identified as not mastered and their related goals can then be used to complete an IEP/ITP with short-term objectives. If the four Xs = ceiling method is used, you will identify up to 24 different objectives for the student and then proceed with the development of specific intervention plans for each item. When the ceiling method is used, the process should be repeated on intervals of not less than 5 or 6 weeks and no more than 10 weeks in order to monitor the student's progress and the effectiveness of the current intervention plan. Repeating this process at the end of the intervention interval will provide documentation of newly mastered objectives and the needed data for adding new objectives to be achieved. These interval evaluations also provide the basis for teams to make relevant adjustments in the intervention plans.

Redefining and Adding Objectives

As noted above, the BOS does not contain every and any objective that may be appropriate for a specific student. The Current Performance Form provides spaces labeled "Individual" within each subscale so that non-BOS objectives can be included. The provision to include these objectives within and across subscales is intended to suggest that evaluators consider the domain goals of each subscale and the developmental or task-analytic attributes of the new objective. You may also find that an existing BOS objective is relevant; however, it may need to be "sliced" into smaller task-analytic steps. Finally, the BOS includes many specific examples of behaviors to add clarification and definition for objectives. Some of these examples may be used as objectives themselves and recorded in the spaces labeled "Individual" on the Current Performance Form.

Using the BOS for Program Placement Decisions

The BOS can be a very helpful tool when considering placement options or changes in placement. With experience, you will begin to recognize patterns in BOS results that vary with characteristics associated with different general intervention needs. For example, students with severe emotional and/or behavioral disorders will typically have a profile with generally low-numbered objectives mastered across all subscales. In other words, if you are using the ceiling method, these students will most likely demonstrate few, if any, mastered objectives above the early 300-level objectives, and the nature of these objectives will suggest a strong need for a highly structured environment with considerable adult-directed activity. Most often these are students for whom special class, special school, and agency settings are recommended. The older students, particularly from middle school and up, with this profile are socially very discrepant from their peers and likely to present significant intervention challenges to mainstream teachers and other traditional regular school-based personnel.

Students with a performance profile that is also generally flat across all subscales, but approaches or includes 200-level objectives will still require significant support; however, many can be successful with some mainstream classroom experiences. Students with uneven profiles, or bounce between subscales (high achievement on one or more subscales and low achievement on others), are usually students who benefit with support in regular schools from special education and other specialist personnel. For example, students with learning disabilities often have objectives that are similar to students with EBD on the Adaptive, Communication, Task, and Personal subscales, while they generally do better on the Self-Management and Interpersonal subscales. Other students, such as those with conduct disorders, may also present bounce between subscales; however, the decisions related to placement may be more directly related to specific items on the Self-Management, Interpersonal, and Personal subscales.

Using the BOS as a Curriculum for Inclusion

The fundamental mission of all intervention programs, whether they are in educational, mental health, juvenile justice, or other community agency settings, is to foster social and emotional skills that will enable recipients to function independently and successfully in natural settings with their peers. The BOS was written specifically for this mission. It presents a "curriculum" of essential competencies that help children and youth to succeed in inclusionary settings. Students who lack proficiency with these skills are likely to have much difficulty in regular classrooms, and at the high school level they are vulnerable to dropping out of school and/or becoming involved with the corrections system or intensive mental health services. Thus, service providers may use the BOS as one tool for planning placement, transition activities, and readiness for inclusion.

Using the Intervention Plan Forms

Individual Intervention Plan Form

The development of detailed intervention plans follows assessment. The BOS includes an Individual Intervention Plan Form that can be used to prepare these intervention plans to achieve short-term objectives (see the Appendix). This comprehensive form is intended to minimize preparation time. It provides areas for all, or most, currently required information on IEP/ITPs, including student and school/agency identification; specific objectives (carried forward from the Current Performance Form); details of the plan; monitoring system; parent, school, and community agency collaboration; and other related services that are being provided.

Essential components of an individual intervention plan should include these elements:

1. Specific goals and objectives from the IEP/ITP

2. Specific beginning and ending dates

3. Names of staff completing and responsible for implementing the plan, including other agency personnel involved

4. Specific content of activities based on assessment data and designed to assist the student achieve the objectives, including:

    Environmental/setting modifications that will be made to accommodate the student's needs

    Antecedent interventions that will be used to teach or elicit the desired behaviors

    Suppressive interventions that will be used if/when inappropriate behavior occurs

    Specific description of, and rationale for, plans that may be at variance with routine program procedures and may require administrative approval

    Name(s) of the person(s) who will be responsible for any specific elements of the plan

5. When suppressive interventions are used (e.g., timeout), the procedures for paired eliciting and reinforcement of desired and incompatible behavior

6. A specific procedure for on-going monitoring of progress toward the objectives and periodic summative evaluation

7. Procedures for sharing the plan's contents with appropriate and permitted others

8. Conditions that may call for amendments or termination of the plan

School-Community Agency Coordinated Intervention Plan

Many of the children and youth with whom the BOS will be used are or will receive services from multiple agencies, including schools. These collaborative interventions are often essential to successful outcomes. The BOS includes a School-Community Agency Coordinated Intervention Plan form (see the Appendix) to help intervention teams focus on specific objectives and coordinate plans that can optimize the activities of the resources from the various agencies involved.

Considerations for Intervention Planning

Successful intervention work is most appropriately measured by its long-term and generalizable results. It is based on a positive and whole-person vision of what an individual can become, not a simple view of eliminating or suppressing unwanted behaviors. It is about prosocial development. It recognizes that all behavior, desirable and undesirable, serves some function for an individual and has a learning history. The functions of behavior are linked to satisfying personal needs. These may be physical needs such as for food, shelter, health, or safety. While care providers must insure that physical needs are met, their primary role is creating optimal developmental or learning environments for the teaching of prosocial skills that enable individuals to meet their emotional and social needs. Thus, the effectiveness of a specific strategy or program is related to the degree to which it responds to the behaviors, characteristics, and needs of individuals.

Functional Analysis

The "behavioral model" provides well-documented and effective procedures for modifying specific behaviors. Careful observations of antecedent and consequent events are a vital consideration in determining triggers and reinforcers for inappropriate behaviors, as well as for monitoring the outcomes of intervention changes in the setting and/or behavioral consequences. The emphasis on "functional assessment" reasserts the importance of considering not only the observable topography of behaviors, but also the "meaning" or purpose of behaviors. This approach provides excellent tools for conducting analyses of specific target behaviors (see Breen & Fiedler, 1996).

The Target Objective Functional Analysis Planning Worksheet (see the Appendix) was developed as a tool for organizing assessment information to help understand student behaviors and to plan and predict the effects of various interventions and placements (Wood & Braaten, 1992). This worksheet and the accompanying Functional Analysis Planning Worksheet Summary, also in the Appendix, are designed to guide users through a problem-solving process beginning with the identification of specific problem behaviors, followed by context analysis, determination of goals and objectives, development and implementation of a plan, and concluding with an evaluation of the intervention.

The dimensions, or cells, of the worksheet are based on the following assumptions about behavior. First, there is a relationship between observed behavior (actions and verbalizations) and accompanying, but hidden, thoughts and feelings which can only be inferred. Second, there is a causal relationship between events which precede (antecedents) and follow (consequences) a behavior. Finally, behaviors occur within a context that includes the student's physical and social environment as well as inferred factors about the student such as the student's sensory acuity, health, motivational state, and personal interpretation of events.

Observable Target Behavior

"Positive" (appropriate) behavior, as well as "negative" (inappropriate) behavior, can be analyzed on the worksheet. Use separate worksheets for contrasting positive and negative behaviors. First describe the *specific observable target behavior(s)* being analyzed in the center circle of the worksheet. Observable behavior includes verbalizations and actions—behavior that can be seen and/or heard—not an interpretation of the behavior. Also include the frequency, persistence, and intensity of the behavior.

Examples of negative behaviors include:

1. For the past month, Sue gets out of her seat without permission an average of 4 times per hour.
2. Bill is late for class 7 times per week.
3. Jorge leaves the classroom 3 times per day.
4. Jill talks out without permission an average of 7 times per hour.
5. Charles hits peers when he does not get his way.
6. Sam is truant from school an average of 4 out of 10 days.
7. Ben threatens and swears at peers on the bus at least twice a week.
8. LaToya sleeps in the second-hour class every day.
9. Harold has not turned in any homework assignments this quarter.

Examples of positive behaviors are:

1. Jane completes all of her math assignments.
2. Mondrel attends school every day.
3. Gene asks for teacher help when he is teased by peers.
4. Maria raises her hand to get permission to speak.
5. Greg asks to speak when he is frustrated.
6. Joan invites timid students to join in class activities.
7. Tom takes a minute and counts to 10 to calm down when he gets upset.

Environmental Antecedents

This cell on the worksheet is used to describe the environmental setting and characteristics or events that are typically observed to be present just before the target behavior occurs. It helps us understand what may be triggering the target behavior. Information is organized to answer the general questions of "Who," "What," "Where," and "When." "Who" factors include persons present, roles modeled, group size, and group history. "What" factors include the activity (required task or other behavior), expectations, or standards for participation and related consequences. "Where" factors include place characteristics such as attributes of the building, grounds, bus, etc. "When" factors include the time of day and sequence location on a schedule of activities. Examples include:

1. The target behavior occurs in the classroom with 26 other students during academic task times, but not during physical education class, art, or lunch times.
2. The target behavior occurs in Mr. G's class, but not in others. Mr. G is very stern and expects all students to be doing the *same* work.
3. The target behavior occurs on the bus when there is no bus assistant. Bill, a neighborhood rival, also rides the bus.
4. The target behavior typically occurs during the 5th and 6th periods of the day no matter what the activity is.
5. The target behavior is less frequent during small-group time.
6. The target behavior occurs in the hall and on the school grounds.

Personal Antecedents

This cell is used to provide background information which helps staff to make inferences about factors the student brings into the situation and that may also help explain the target behavior. Measures of achievement or intelligence provide *estimates* of learning and level of development. General measures of "self-concept," including formal inventories and self-reports, provide another basis for estimates of the student's responses in specific situations. Indirect measures of health or physical, sensory, and cognitive functioning can contribute to inferences about the student's responsiveness. Information about the family and the involvement of the juvenile court or social service agencies can provide indicators of additional factors that predict responses. Also included in this cell are inferences by staff about the student's "expectancies," "motivation," and goals or "chosen role."

Learner self-expectancies

Expectancies of competence and success can be inferred from self-reports and compared with staff observations of performance in the same or similar situations. For example, anticipation of success or failure in academic classes, sports, music, art, mechanics, or social situations may represent a "self-fulfilling prophecy" or provide very useful information about the student's perceived competencies on various tasks and in various settings. Examples include:

1. Susan eagerly enters athletic contests with confidence, but resists spelling bees.

2. Sam readily contributes to small-group social discussions, but will not make contributions to discussions on class assignments.

Learner motivation

Student motivation must be considered separately from expectations regarding performance competence. Students may be very capable of performing desired behaviors, but for various reasons, not willing to do so. Further, expectation of failure may undermine willingness to perform despite desire for the reward available to those who perform successfully. Staff judgments about motivation are inferred from the same kind of data as inferences about student expectancies.

Learner long-range goals or "chosen role"

Patterns of behavior developed in younger students that occur consistently across different situations may have been shaped by life experiences. Older students frequently behave in accordance with a chosen set of goals, or role, that is heavily influenced by peers and factors outside of school. Negatively oriented, deviant, or alienated role models may also influence the behavior of students. Efforts to behave in a manner consistent with a "chosen role" may dictate stereotypic responses to authority. Or, events that arouse anxiety or fear in the student may override the student's desired, but conflicting, expectancies and motives such as achievement and compliance. Further, staff need to be aware of distinctions between situational responses and behavior patterns or roles such as "happy," "clown," "jock," "flirt," "punk," "loner," "gang member," "drug user."

Environmental Consequences

The focus in this cell is on how the environment and persons in it *respond* to the student's behavior. How does the target behavior change others' responses to it (the "Who," "What," "Where," and "When" factors)? Do the consequences or responses to the behavior appear to be reinforcing or punishing? Compare the student's verbalized evaluation of the consequences to his/her behavior with observed effects on the behavior. Increases in the frequency, persistence, or intensity of the behavior indicate that the consequences are reinforcing. Punishing consequences lead to decreases in the behavior.

Personal Thoughts and Feelings

This cell is focused on the "meaning" of the target behavior and its consequences for the student. It is important to distinguish between what students say about the meaning of their behavior and the inferences about thoughts and feelings derived from staff observations. Sensitive observers often find differences between what students say about thoughts and feelings and their nonverbal actions, such as posture and expression. In this cell, inferences from self-reports and actions are interpreted and recorded as hypotheses about the "feeling tone" that accompanies the student's target behavior(s). Some information gathered may suggest a relationship not only to the target behavior, but also to that behavior's effects on the environment and others (how the student "feels" about the behavior and how he/she thinks or wants others to "feel" about it). The rewarding or punishing nature of consequences that are observed may be managed in ways by students that are in conflict with expected effects– "punishing" consequences may be interpreted as "deserved" or even as rewarding by some students, and vice versa. For example, in extreme cases, a student who has experienced physical or sexual abuse may seek punishment while reporting it as "painful," or a gang member may reject rewards because accepting them is disapproved of by the gang.

The Functional Analysis Planning Worksheet Summary (see the Appendix) is a convenient form for recording conclusions from the functional analysis process and briefly listing details of intervention and evaluation plans. The process should be repeated for each new objective and in particular when current intervention plans are unsuccessful.

Developmental Assessment

The BOS was constructed from an integration of developmental and task analysis concepts. Behavioral psychology provides extremely practical tools for assessing and modifying specific target behaviors. Task analysis procedures are helpful for defining explicit learning sequences. However, behavioral technology can fail to provide a contextual framework for understanding and selecting developmentally appropriate target objectives. For example, school personnel and others commonly, and understandably, are concerned about aggression and seek interventions to manage aggressive behaviors. Too often the result is a properly intended, but short-sighted and punishment-based, "curriculum" of compliance and control, rather than prosocial development. While it is certainly important to use potent and effective interventions to inhibit aggressive behaviors, short-term gain and long-term success may depend on intervention programs built on a foundation from developmental psychology.

Child development theory and research provide a conceptual model for designing intervention programs that are based on "normal" developmental patterns and help practitioners to focus on a growth-based, rather than pathology-based, approach to working with children and youth. This perspective takes into consideration that, while all behavior patterns are learned and individuals vary widely in their responses to experiences, they also share common basic needs and develop in generally predictable ways. The following intervention planning guidelines come from the child development literature and were prepared to accompany the BOS. For a more detailed discussion, see Jones and Jones (1995), Lipsitz (1980), Vernon (1993), Vernon and Al-Mabuk (1995), and Wood et al. (1996).

The 300-level BOS objectives address skills that are typically mastered by children before they enter school. The basic developmental issues or needs of this age include trust, pleasure, support, and structure. The perspective of little children is very "me" centered. Healthy development depends on daily affirmations of feeling "significant" or "worthwhile" to someone who is important (e.g., parents) in environments that provide high levels of pleasurable experiences with few opportunities to fail (structure). During these first years, exploration and play are the child's developmental tasks with little consideration for the needs of others. The foundation for self-control is also established in learning to manage bodily functions and to respond appropriately to the word "no." The implications for intervention suggest a role for the adult that I call a "benevolent dictator." This role, like that of a parent, involves creating environments where each day the student experiences affirmations of "significance," predictable structured routine, and much repetition with pleasurable and successful activities. The adult determines the basic agenda, provides continuous supervision, manages the setting, controls movement, and limits the student's choices. Social competencies are learned by direct instruction and from prosocial models. Reinforcers are tangible and provided frequently. New and challenging skills are introduced thoughtfully and paced to ensure early successes. Inappropriate behaviors are always confronted, but viewed as opportunities for teaching rather than merely to be punished. At this level, the adult assumes responsibility for creating and orchestrating the conditions for prosocial development. While the student may "know" what or what not to do, it is not assumed that he/she has mastered the intra- or interpersonal competencies to succeed without adult structure.

The 200-level BOS objectives address skills that are typically acquired during the elementary school years. During these years children learn that they are not the center of the universe and they become attentive and sensitive to "others." Developmental tasks include expanding personal and communication skills along with learning how to become a group member. The basic issues involve experiencing "competence," that is, how to get one's needs met in ways that are valued by others. This means that the student is able to apply social skills in different groups and settings that are not always carefully orchestrated by adults. Peers acquire strong influence on each other's behavior. While this is a common source of consternation for adults, it is critical to recognize this as a "normal" process and suggests that the adult role now shift from "benevolent dictator" to "group leader." The group is a natural and important part of intervention programs at this level, and students who are yet unskilled will have many problems to address. The leader role is intended to emphasize that it is still very important for the adult to "be in charge." However, students will need many guided opportunities for an expanded array of choices. They will need guidance in using problem-solving skills, contributing to groups, practicing social competencies, and responding constructively to peer feedback. High levels of success continue to be critical because being perceived as "competent" at something valued by others is essential to one's perception of becoming a group member. Intervention programs continue to require a high level of structure with both consistency and repetition as students shift from the "me" focus of early childhood to working in groups with others. Decision-making and problem-solving skills are learned through expanded privileges, along with the acceptance of personal responsibility that comes from logical consequences. Frequent reinforcement is also still important; however, the emphasis shifts from tangible rewards to verbal and social contingencies. Interventions at this level require a delicate balance between adult-imposed structure and sufficient autonomy for students to have experience making decisions and learning from their consequences.

The 100-level BOS objectives reflect skills that are associated with early adolescence through young adulthood. Adolescence presents an array of important and well-known developmental tasks. These include defining oneself in relation to characteristics of others, affiliating with or "belonging" to a preference group (a real sense of "us"), and acquiring experience with "personal power." Personal power means gradually separating from adult controls and feeling empowered to make decisions about matters that are thought to be important. Basic issues that need to be addressed are applying one's skills in new situations and self-monitoring. As individuals continue to develop and master expanded intra- and interpersonal competencies, the role of the adult shifts again. The adult must take more of a guidance and facilitator role. Interventions include "normalized" expectations with a future orientation, individual and group problem solving and decision making, and broader choices and opportunities along with inclusion in the mainstream school and community life with peers.

Intervention at all developmental levels should be based on valid and on-going assessment procedures. Changes in intervention plans should be based on the effectiveness of the plans along with consideration of the student's developmental or maturational growth.

Using the BOS for Individual and Program Evaluation

Monitoring, or charting, and reporting intervention outcomes are widely regarded as essential components of best practice standards and are required under governmental regulations for most service providers, including special education.

Progress Monitoring

Professionals use a variety of methods to monitor progress including target behavior graphing from direct observations, logs, self-reports from interviews, checklists, and permanent product records (tangible items produced by the student). The intervention plan forms discussed previously include options for indicating the appropriate monitoring method that will be used for each objective.

The Daily Monitoring Record can be used to chart performance (see the Appendix). This form provides a time-saving method to indicate that performance criteria were, or were not, met on a specific day. The method is referred to as "frequency count by day" (FCD) and was developed because large numbers of objectives may need to be monitored concurrently, which is a very difficult and time-intensive task. This approach may be less accurate than event charting from structured observations; however, when used over a period of weeks and mastery criteria are high, it tends to offer an efficient and reliable approach to monitoring progress. In addition, the Team Meeting Notes and Interagency Meeting Notes can be used to document staff meetings regarding the effectiveness of intervention plans (see the Appendix).

When progress is slow or change occurs in small increments, one may need to use the more precise measures from structured observations that can be recorded on the Target Behavior Performance Chart (see the Appendix). This method uses a "frequency count by event" (FCE) observed. While this method provides the most accurate data on change, it is also the most time intensive and often not possible or practical. One technique for obtaining this type of information, while reducing observation time, is called "time sampling" (TS). This method requires that users describe the process used to record data including the number and duration of observation intervals.

Progress Reporting

Progress reporting is a critical component of all intervention plans. It is vital that the students themselves get feedback and know that they are making progress. Parents and all other concerned school and professional personnel need to be aware of gains that are being made, and if none, then what adjustments in the intervention plans may be considered. Progress reports may be in a variety of forms including graphs and narrative documents, but should address the specific objectives that the student is expected to achieve. The BOS includes a Behavioral Progress Report (see the Appendix), which can be used to share current performance data as well as other relevant information with parents and others. The progress reports should reflect information gathered from all personnel who are directly involved with the implementation of intervention plans and should be provided on frequent intervals.

Federal regulations require that special education IEPs be reviewed at least annually. Other disciplines may have similar requirements. The BOS also includes an Annual Progress Summary Form (see the Appendix). This form can be used for maintaining a cumulative list of current-year objectives within selected intervals (e.g., 6, 12, or 18 weeks) and an option to note which objectives were actually achieved. Collectively, the BOS process, with its related forms, provides users with a documentation system that includes assessment of current levels of performance and the history of intervention plans and outcomes.

Program Evaluation

Quality programs are recognized by a variety of indicators, of which the most important is the achievement outcomes by the children and youth who are served. The BOS provides one convenient data source for this purpose, which can be accomplished by aggregating information from the Annual Progress Summary Form and preparing statistical summaries to include along with other program information.

BOS Research

Limited data exists which does indicate that the BOS has strong characteristics for use as a rating scale and predictive potential for assisting in making placement decisions (Braaten & Bloomberg, 1989). Statistical studies were conducted over a 2-year period including interrater reliability, test-retest reliability, content validity, sequence validity, factor analysis, and correlations with the "Child Behavior Checklist" (Achenbach, 1991).The studies included approximately 200 students with emotional and behavioral disorders and 100 students with learning disabilities, ranging in age from kindergarten through high school. All of the subjects were receiving special education services in resource rooms, special classes, or special schools. No studies have been conducted with general student populations. The available results indicate acceptable to high reliability levels across the subscales and predictive potential for identifying appropriate service settings. The studies did show that a rating scale procedure for the BOS resulted in correlations of approximately .90 or higher with direct daily observation procedures across the subscales. One note of caution: The available data, while very encouraging, is based on a relatively small population from one urban city and additional research is necessary before any generalizations may be made.

In Brief

The BOS is a task-analyzed sequence of behavioral objectives, organized along with concepts from child and adolescent development. It may be used as simply an inventory of skills or as an integral part of a comprehensive process for IEP/ITP planning, on-going progress monitoring, intervention planning, and as a guide for organizing program services. It should be used by individuals who have direct experiences with the youth being evaluated and based upon direct observations with minimal interpretation of behaviors.

REFERENCES

Achenbach, T.M. (1991). *Manual for Child Behavior Checklist/4-18 & 1991 Profile.* Burlington, VT: Department of Psychiatry, University of Vermont.

Braaten, S.L., & Bloomberg, L. (1989). Effectiveness of Level IV/V Programs in the Minneapolis Public Schools: Phase 1. Report to Minnesota Department of Education, Unique Learner Section, Grant # 052-EFF-089.

Breen, M.J., & Fiedler, C.R. (1996). *Behavioral approach to the assessment of youth with emotional/behavioral disorders.* Austin, TX: Pro-Ed.

Jones, V.F., & Jones, L.S. (1995). *Comprehensive classroom management: Creating positive learning environments for all students (4th ed).* Boston: Allyn & Bacon.

Lipsitz, J. (1980). *Growing up forgotten: A review of research and programs concerning early adolescence.* New Brunswick, NJ: Transaction Books.

Vernon, A. (1993). *Developmental assessment and intervention with children and adolescents.* Alexandria, VA: American Counseling Association.

Vernon, A., & Al-Mabuk, R.H. (1995). *What growing up is all about: A parent's guide to child and adolescent development.* Champaign, IL: Research Press.

Wood, F.H., & Braaten, S.L. (1992). *Using the analysis planning worksheet.* Unpublished manuscript.

Wood, M.M. (1981). *Developmental therapy source books* (Vols. 1 and 2). Austin, TX: Pro-Ed.

Wood, M.M., Davis, K.R., Swindle, L., & Quirk, C. (1996). *Developmental therapy-Developmental teaching: Fostering social-emotional competence in troubled children and youth.* Austin, TX: Pro-Ed.

BOS Subscale Definitions and Long-Term Goals by Level

Adaptive Behaviors

Definition: The student demonstrates appropriate behaviors in response to routine expectations and rules and modifies behaviors appropriately in response to new situations and circumstances.

Long-Term Goals

Level 3
1. The student will attend school regularly.
2. The student will participate in routine school activities.

Level 2
1. The student will demonstrate sustained attention to tasks in group-focused activities.
2. The student will contribute to group success by following group rules and responsibilities.

Level 1
1. The student will follow known rules and respect new authority figures without continuous supervision.
2. The student will demonstrate capability to engage in concentrated involvement in an activity.
3. The student will respond to new life experiences with constructive behaviors.

Self-Management Behaviors

Definition: The student demonstrates the skills that enable him/her to respond to challenging experiences with self-control and seeks to be successful.

Long-Term Goals

Level 3
1. The student will attempt structured new experiences and seek success.
2. The student will differentiate between intentional and unintentional acts and accept responsibility for own behaviors.
3. The student will accept and utilize adult help and directions.

Level 2
1. The student will demonstrate the ability to view situations from another person's perspective.
2. The student will demonstrate comfort and satisfaction in group-focused experiences.

Level 1
1. The student will demonstrate basic problem-solving skills and effectively manage personal affairs.
2. The student will demonstrate an understanding of personal goals and the ability to formulate realistic expectations for self.
3. The student will develop a personal plan for continuing education and growth.

Communication Behaviors

Definition: The student demonstrates the verbal and nonverbal skills that enable him/her to appropriately meet his/her own needs and to affect others in positive ways.

Long-Term Goals

Level 3
1. The student will use verbal language to get adults to respond to personal needs and wishes.

2. The student will use words and behaviors to affect others in positive and appropriate ways.

Level 2
1. The student will use words to express oneself appropriately in group situations.

2. The student will use words and behaviors to contribute to group success.

Level 1
1. The student will use words to establish and/or enrich social relationships, independent of adult structure.

2. The student will demonstrate ability to appropriately express personal opinions and needs and to recognize those communicated by others.

Interpersonal Behaviors

Definition: The student demonstrates the skills that enable him/her to interact with others in social and task situations in ways that meet personal and interdependent needs and that contribute to a sense of belonging.

Long-Term Goals

Level 3
1. The student will participate in selected adult-structured activities with other students.

2. The student will demonstrate knowledge of and compliance with basic social rules for constructive interactions.

Level 2
1. The student will participate in and contribute to the success of interdependent activities focused on collective group goals.

2. The student will demonstrate knowledge of individuals' differences and how individuals' behaviors contribute to or interfere with personal and group success.

Level 1
1. The student will spontaneously participate in group tasks and social activities.

2. The student will initiate and maintain positive relationships, independent of adult structure.

Task Behaviors

Definition: The student engages in learning tasks and activities that are routinely assigned by the teacher and for which grades or credits are received. These behaviors include preparing for a learning activity, attempting assignments, and demonstrating growth.

Long-Term Goals

Level 3
1. The student will attempt assigned individualized tasks.
2. The student will accept and seek adult assistance.
3. The student will minimally participate in group tasks.

Level 2
1. The student will routinely participate in group-structured academic tasks.
2. The student will follow written instructions for academic assignments.
3. The student will accept instruction and follow directions from different teachers for different classes.

Level 1
1. The student will routinely work on and complete assignments in classes that simulate mainstream classes.
2. The student will be prepared and come to classes with appropriate materials.
3. The student will complete, with passing grades, at least 2 hours per day of mainstream classes.

Personal Behaviors

Definition: The student engages in dialog with a counseling adult, permitting the adult to assist the student in resolving personal issues, developing personal skills, and building a sense of self-worth.

Note: "Counselor" in this document refers to an adult who is in the role, or circumstance, of providing services relating to the objectives. This person may be a social worker, psychologist, special education teacher, or other trained adult.

Long-Term Goals

Level 3
1. The student will attend to and accept input/feedback from an adult.
2. The student will demonstrate a developing trust with selected adults by responding appropriately to help that is offered.
3. The student will accurately label personal feelings to an adult.

Level 2
1. The student will verbally demonstrate knowledge of the relationship among feelings, behaviors, and consequences.
2. The student will verbally demonstrate knowledge or ability to clarify personal expectations of others.
3. The student will verbally demonstrate ability to identify or describe the feelings of others.

Level 1
1. The student will compare different values and clarify personal priorities.
2. The student will develop realistic personal expectations.
3. The student will assert personal needs and feelings while respecting the rights of others.

Behavioral

Objective

Sequence

Adaptive Behaviors

DEFINITION

The student demonstrates appropriate behaviors in response to routine expectations and rules and modifies behaviors appropriately in response to new situations and circumstances.

LEVEL 3 Long-Term Goals—Adaptive Behaviors

1. The student will attend school regularly.
2. The student will participate in routine school activities.

Objectives: The student will...

301. physically or verbally demonstrate an awareness of events occurring around him/her by looking in the direction of the events or responding in any manner.

> EXAMPLES
> 1. looks at a person who walks into the room
> 2. looks in the direction of people talking
> 3. looks away when called on to respond in a group

302. attend 75% of the school days during the marking period.
(Note: This objective does not mean attend all classes or all day.)

> EXAMPLES
> 1. comes to school on 23 out of 30 consecutive school days (6 weeks)
> 2. comes to school on 34 out of 45 consecutive school days (9 weeks)
> 3. comes to school on 45 out of 60 consecutive school days (12 weeks)

303. remember routine daily schedule without reminders.

> EXAMPLES
> 1. when asked, correctly tells the order of classes during the day
> 2. when asked, correctly tells what time a specific class begins
> 3. correctly tells which scheduled and/or elective classes he/she has on which days of the week

304. comply with written bus-riding rules.

EXAMPLES
1. rides the school bus without receiving a "bus behavior report" for 27 out of 30 (34 out of 45) consecutive school days
2. receives "bus tickets" (reinforcers/points) for a.m. and p.m. rides
3. receives a complimentary note from the bus driver about behavior on the bus

305. arrive at school on time, if not transported by the school bus.

EXAMPLES
1. if student walks to school, arrives at the classroom by the beginning of the first instructional period (does not include breakfast if offered)
2. if student rides city bus, arrives at the classroom by the beginning of the first instructional period (does not include breakfast if offered)
3. if student is on alternate schedule, either from another school or on a reduced day, arrives at the office by the appointed time

306. bring to school or display no materials which disrupt the routine classroom operation or distract his/her attention from assigned activities or tasks.

EXAMPLES
1. complies with school rule: do not bring any objects such as radios, tape players, toys, games, animals, or candy, without first receiving permission from the teacher, parent, and bus driver
2. when given permission, uses an object only during times agreed to by the teacher

307. use non-classroom areas and facilities within the building appropriately.

EXAMPLES
1. walks quietly and orderly in the hall
2. sits in assigned area at lunch
3. uses lavatory with permission
4. enters office or hall only with escort or on a pass
5. sits quietly on a chair in the office while waiting for _____
6. sits in assigned area during assemblies and attends to the activity or program
7. uses student recreation/lounge equipment and property appropriately
8. obeys rule: do not enter restricted areas of building
9. obeys smoking policy

308. attend scheduled classes or activities on time and remain for the duration.

EXAMPLES
1. when permitted, walks promptly to appropriate room arriving on time for the beginning of class/activity and remains for the duration
2. maintains appropriate self-control of behavior in order to be ready for the next activity, rather than set up consequences for misconduct as a means to avoid the activity
3. refrains from requesting to see the nurse or other staff as a means to avoid an activity
4. remains in class, with staff support, when frustrated or angry, rather than walk out of the room

309. remain in school for its duration daily.

EXAMPLES
1. stays at school until dismissed by the teacher at the end of the day
2. if student has doctor's appointment or other legitimate excuse, stays until dismissed by the teacher, counselor, or administrator
3. if student "skips" from a class, returns to the program within 20 minutes and remains until dismissed at the end of the day

310. attend non-academic activities such as assemblies, gym, field trips, etc.

EXAMPLES
1. follows a direction to go to the gym class, assembly, or other activity, but may choose not to participate
2. saves and spends points to go on a field trip

311. participate in non-academic activities 70% or more of the time of each activity period.

EXAMPLE
1. when directed or with encouragement, participates in the structured activity for at least 21 out of 30 minutes or 35 out of 50 minutes–prompts and redirects may by used

312. accept or respond to changes in routine class activities without emotional outbursts when reasons are explained.

EXAMPLES
1. stops working on an assignment to attend to someone who enters the room to make an announcement to the group
2. accepts the teacher's decision to change gym plan to an inside game because it is raining
3. responds to a request from the counselor to go with the counselor from a favored activity
4. agrees to participate in an alternate activity when the regular teacher is absent
5. stops work on one assignment and begins work on a different subject when class period ends and new one begins

313. arrive at the school physically clean.

EXAMPLES
1. bathes daily–hands, face, hair, and fingernails are clean
2. brushes teeth daily

314. try again when faced with disappointment or failure in a structured activity, given reassurance, an explanation, or encouragement from an adult.

EXAMPLES
1. after making a mistake on an art or crafts project, makes a correction and resumes the task
2. after striking out in a softball game, continues to play
3. after having a game piece taken by opponent in chess game, continues to play
4. after failing to earn all possible points during a marking period, continues trying to earn points in the next period
5. after missing a basket in a game, continues to play
6. chooses another elective class if the first and/or second choice are already full

315. follow rules and directions when on field trips or other school activities away from the school building.

EXAMPLES
1. remains with the group
2. earns all points by complying with stated rules and directions
3. if uncertain about rules or expectations, asks the teacher

316. attempt new tasks or activities, with adult support or encouragement.

EXAMPLES
1. begins work on a new math skill after instructions have been given
2. participates in role play for a new social skill
3. signs up for an elective class in a new content area
4. participates in a new gym game
5. learns a new computer skill

317. eat at a reasonable pace and clean the eating area.

EXAMPLES
1. begins eating promptly when served and takes time to chew food between bites
2. does not "pick at" or play with food
3. finishes meal and cleans up within time provided

318. wear appropriate and clean clothing to school.

EXAMPLES
1. wears clothes appropriate for the temperature
2. wears clothes that have been washed
3. wears clothes without writing or pictures that are of a sexual, racial, gang, or otherwise offensive reference
4. wears clothes that are within reasonable boundaries of sexual propriety

319. attend school daily during the marking period, excluding absences excused for illness or other valid reasons.

EXAMPLES
1. comes to the classroom 27 of 30; 40.5 of 45; or 45 of 60 consecutive school days
2. when absent, provides a document of legitimate excuse such as a note from parent or doctor

320. follow common-sense safety rules and avoid dangerous situations.

EXAMPLES
1. walks carefully on snowy or ice-covered sidewalk
2. walks in the hallway
3. stays with the group on field trips
4. does not run into the street
5. does not climb on furniture
6. does not crawl up onto high objects
7. follows safety rules for use of tools or equipment provided in classes such as shop, sewing, kitchen, science
8. does not slam doors
9. walks up and down stairs
10. avoids situations where there is extreme conflict with others that may involve physical violence
11. follows rules for using pool table or other recreational equipment

LEVEL 2 Long-Term Goals—Adaptive Behaviors

1. The student will demonstrate sustained attention to tasks in group-focused activities.
2. The student will contribute to group success by following group rules and responsibilities.

Objectives: The student will...

221. spontaneously participate in routine class activities.

EXAMPLES
1. begins work on assignments after directions have been given to the group without direct personal prompt
2. begins art project after materials have been handed out without direct personal prompt
3. does warm-up gym exercises without an individual prompt
4. volunteers feedback to an individual during group time

222. spontaneously participate in non-academic activities previously avoided, without adult cues.

EXAMPLES
1. volunteers to do role play in social skills class
2. participates in gym, group feedback, or other low-preference routine activity/class that has been avoided
3. participates in home room activities and discussions

223. walk through halls appropriately with hall pass.

EXAMPLES
1. walks quietly and directly to destination
2. shows pass when requested by an adult
3. responds appropriately to interactions initiated by an adult
4. avoids peer interactions with potential conflict

224. change from one activity to another, without resistance or emotional outbursts, when the time for change is announced.

EXAMPLE
1. puts away materials/books promptly and prepares to begin the next activity without personal reminders

225. self-select appropriate structured or approved activities when assigned tasks are completed and not disrupt others.

EXAMPLES
1. takes out unfinished assignments to work on after completing current task
2. gets a book to read or other approved material without interfering with other students

226. demonstrate socially acceptable table manners.

EXAMPLES
1. uses fork, spoon, and knife appropriately
2. uses napkin
3. uses "Please" to have condiments passed
4. cleans up area without prompts
5. remains seated while others finish eating

227. complete individual and/or group tasks assigned by an adult.
(Note: See Task 307 for academic assignments.)

EXAMPLES
1. participates in gym for the duration of the class period
2. finishes art project assigned within time provided
3. finishes sewing project within the duration of the class periods provided
4. participates in group feedback throughout the discussion period

228. return borrowed property promptly and in good condition.

EXAMPLES
1. returns reference book at the end of the class
2. returns tape player used during "free time"
3. puts game pieces back into box and returns to appropriate storage area
4. returns borrowed pen or pencil to the teacher at the end of class

LEVEL 1 Long-Term Goals—Adaptive Behaviors

1. The student will follow known rules and respect new authority figures without continuous supervision.
2. The student will demonstrate capability to engage in concentrated involvement in an activity.
3. The student will respond to new life experiences with constructive behaviors.

Objectives: The student will...

129. demonstrate the ability to wait for rewards offered by adults that may take several days or weeks to obtain.

> EXAMPLES
> 1. saves points for a field trip that is one or more weeks away
> 2. saves points for one week or longer for an item in the school store
> 3. negotiates a contract and meets its terms for one week or more

130. bring required materials for assignments to class.

> EXAMPLE
> 1. has pencil, paper, and/or other needed materials without reminders

131. begin, attend, and participate regularly in part-time mainstream classes, with support from special education staff or other resource staff.

> EXAMPLES
> 1. attends class(es) scheduled in neighborhood or vocational school daily
> 2. carries monitoring note from regular teacher indicating appropriate participation

132. accept and use support from mainstream resources when offered, independent of outreach provided by special/alternative program staff.

> EXAMPLES
> 1. asks regular school social worker, counselor, or special education teacher for help with a concern and follows guidance given
> 2. responds appropriately when approached by mainstream staff regarding a concern
> 3. agrees to meet regularly with mainstream staff to monitor progress/performance

133. successfully complete mainstream class(es) with passing grade(s).

> EXAMPLE
> 1. completes quarter/trimester/semester of non-special education class(es) with passing grade(s)

Self-Management Behaviors

DEFINITION

The student demonstrates the skills that enable him/her to respond to challenging experiences with self-control and seeks to be successful.

LEVEL 3 Long-Term Goals—Self-Management Behaviors

1. The student will attempt structured new experiences and seek success.
2. The student will differentiate between intentional and unintentional acts and accept responsibility for own behaviors.
3. The student will accept and utilize adult help and directions.

Objectives: The student will...

301. respond independently to materials for amusement such as games, puzzles, or objects intended for play and self-entertainment. The focus is on self-entertainment, not necessarily the intended function of the object(s).

EXAMPLES
1. given coloring markers and art paper, colors in a design without continued adult direction
2. given a set of checkers, builds a castle
3. looks at a magazine

302. appear alert and able to focus attention on activities.

EXAMPLES
1. is not drowsy or sleeping in school
2. is sufficiently calm (not excessively hyper) to respond to routine verbal commands
3. is not preoccupied by daydreaming
4. is not demonstrating behavior indicating hallucinations
5. is free from the disabling effects of prescription and/or illicit drugs
6. takes prescribed medication with adult supervision

303. bring no weapons or potential weapons to school 100% of the time.

> EXAMPLE
> 1. acknowledges rule and does not bring knives, chains, sticks, guns (lethal, BB, or toy), explosives, martial arts objects, or any other object intended or otherwise capable of inflicting injury

304. use amusement materials appropriately according to their intended function.

> EXAMPLES
> 1. works a crossword puzzle or other paper-and-pencil game
> 2. plays a table game using pieces appropriately and follows the rules
> 3. uses ping-pong paddles only for ping-pong
> 4. uses art materials appropriately
> 5. plays with an electronic game

305. wait or take turns when directed without physical intervention–verbal prompts may be used.

> EXAMPLES
> 1. follows verbal direction to take turns shooting baskets
> 2. waits until called to pick up lunch at the counter
> 3. stays in assigned place in line
> 4. stays seated until called on to spend points at the class/school store

306. use classroom equipment and property appropriately, when provided by an adult, without abuse, and return to proper place.

> EXAMPLES
> 1. does not deface or damage school books
> 2. returns book to proper place when finished
> 3. treats computer disks carefully and returns to teacher
> 4. follows rules for use of student recreation equipment
> 5. does not deface desk or classroom furniture

307. accept positive or friendly physical contact from others.

> EXAMPLES
> 1. responds to extended hand by shaking appropriately
> 2. smiles when complimented with pat on the back

308. touch others in ways that are appropriate for the school, community, or home.

> EXAMPLES
> 1. refrains from poking, shoving, pinching, or clinging
> 2. refrains from provocative touch with opposite sex
> 3. expresses positive messages physically by appropriate pat, handshake, or "high five"

309. refrain from stealing.

> SELF-EXPLANATORY

310. respond when angry without hitting, kicking, pushing, spitting at people, or having to be physically restrained.

> EXAMPLE
> 1. may yell, swear, or threaten when angry, but refrains from any physically assaultive behaviors

311. recognize and display positive regard for others' possessions.

> EXAMPLES
> 1. asks permission to borrow another's property
> 2. returns property in the same condition it was received
> 3. refrains from going into another's desk without permission
> 4. does not pass borrowed property on to another person without permission

312. accept verbal cue from an adult for removal from a situation or to counseling when angry or upset.

> EXAMPLES
> 1. responds promptly to verbal command to move physically from the group situation to own desk
> 2. goes to the office from the class to cool down when directed
> 3. agrees to accompany the teacher to meet with the counselor or administrator
> 4. agrees to go directly to meet with the counselor when suggested

313. respond when angry without abuse of or damage to property.

> EXAMPLES
> 1. refrains from throwing chairs or other objects, slamming doors, hitting walls/windows when angry, without being physically restrained
> 2. refrains from destroying own work or property when upset

314. accept and respond appropriately to directions from substitute teacher, given structure provided by other permanent staff.

> EXAMPLE
> 1. follows substitute teacher's directions respectfully when other permanent staff are present

315. respond when angry without verbal threats of intent to harm someone, peer or adult.

> EXAMPLE
> 1. expresses feelings of anger, such as "You make me mad," without making direct or indirect statements intending to threaten the individual(s) with whom he/she is angry

316. walk to timeout room or other designated area when directed, without being physically moved by an adult.

> EXAMPLES
> 1. obeys verbal command to go to timeout, without physical intervention by any adult
> 2. leaves area and goes directly to the office when directed
> 3. responds to the verbal command to go to timeout, without a contingent threat of a suspension or police call

LEVEL 2 Long-Term Goals—Self-Management Behaviors

1. The student will demonstrate the ability to view situations from another person's perspective.
2. The student will demonstrate comfort and satisfaction in group-focused experiences.

Objectives: The student will...

217. work or play without interfering or disrupting the work of others.

> EXAMPLES
> 1. works on an independent assignment for the duration of the class time without disrupting other students
> 2. finds another accepted activity without disrupting others when finished with an assignment

218. refrain from inappropriate behavior or breaking group rules when others in the group are losing control, with adult verbal support.

> EXAMPLES
> 1. remains seated or quiet as directed when another student is behaving inappropriately
> 2. refrains from verbal or other behaviors that may reinforce another's misbehavior, when directed by an adult

219. respond to deliberate peer provocation with self-control by ignoring it or requesting adult intervention.

> EXAMPLES
> 1. walks away from a peer who is calling him/her names
> 2. asks an adult to intervene with a bothersome peer

220. respond when angry or upset by initiating self-removal from the situation and/or appropriately seeking adult support.

EXAMPLES
1. requests to see the counselor for help with a problem in class
2. requests to be taken to timeout room/area when upset and needs to cool off
3. requests to talk to the administrator when he/she feels that a staff person has been unfair

221. accept adult help in a crisis when offered.

EXAMPLES
1. follows cue from the teacher to calm down when upset and listens to supportive feedback or guidance
2. agrees, with prompt, to see the counselor for help with the problem

222. given a classroom job, fulfill responsibilities as expected, with direct adult supervision.

EXAMPLES
1. given a job of student attendance aid, complies with the job description and accepts feedback about performance from an adult
2. given a job to clean the blackboard, fulfills responsibility at the appropriate time
3. given a job to feed classroom pets, fulfills responsibility
4. given a job to operate audiovisual equipment, fulfills responsibility as instructed

223. seek adult help in personal and/or group crisis.

EXAMPLES
1. asks to see the counselor for help with a problem at home
2. asks an adult to intervene in a problem with peers to help resolve the issue

224. maintain personal control and routinely comply with established procedures in group situations without reminders.

EXAMPLES
1. follows classroom rules and expectations without reminders, such as going directly to seat upon arriving at class
2. walks quietly and in a line in the hall
3. cleans up after self in the lunchroom
4. remains seated and quiet in assemblies without reminders

225. demonstrate problem-solving skills, with adult assistance.

EXAMPLES
1. suggests possible solutions for the group to decide what game to play in gym when students do not agree
2. offers suggestion during group time for taking turns using school equipment

Level 1 Long-Term Goals—Self-Management Behaviors

1. The student will demonstrate basic problem-solving skills and effectively manage personal affairs.
2. The student will demonstrate an understanding of personal goals and the ability to formulate realistic expectations for self.
3. The student will develop a personal plan for continuing education and growth.

Objectives: The student will...

126. given a job, fulfill described responsibilities as expected, with minimal adult supervision.

EXAMPLES
1. collects lunch count each morning and delivers it to the office at a specified time
2. collects classroom attendance each morning and delivers it to the office at a specified time
3. given the job, delivers a message to the office directly and returns promptly to class
4. given instruction, assists selected peer with tutoring

127. maintain self-control when faced with disappointment, frustration, or failure, without adult intervention.

EXAMPLES
1. remains calm after receiving a low grade and resumes work
2. remains calm after his/her team loses a game in physical education class
3. willingly chooses a different elective class/activity when first choice is already filled
4. remains calm and does participate in a game when not selected for a preferred team

128. obey new or temporary authority figure, without the presence of other permanent staff.

EXAMPLES
1. readily accepts and follows directions from other staff covering the classroom
2. accepts and follows directions from an itinerant teacher
3. accepts and follows directions from a substitute teacher

129. use personal skills to solve problems, without reliance on adult assistance, except when necessary.

> EXAMPLES
> 1. initiates suggestion for solving a problem with a classmate
> 2. during group time, offers a suggestion to a peer for handling a problem with another student or adult
> 3. asks for, or agrees to participate in, a peer mediation session

130. demonstrate knowledge of future rewards for personal goals and the determination to continue working toward them.

> EXAMPLES
> 1. discusses mainstream classes he/she wants to take
> 2. discusses plans to graduate from school
> 3. discusses career or work goals and skills that will be needed

Communication Behaviors

DEFINITION

The student demonstrates the verbal and nonverbal
skills that enable him/her to appropriately meet
his/her own needs and to affect others in positive ways.

LEVEL 3 Long-Term Goals—Communication Behaviors

1. The student will use verbal language to get adults to respond
   to personal needs and wishes.
2. The student will use words and behaviors to affect others
   in positive and appropriate ways.

Objectives: The student will...

301. answer an adult's or another student's verbal request with recognizable
and meaningful words.

> EXAMPLES
>   1. when asked a question, responds with intelligible words
>   2. responds in meaningful phrases or sentences

302. verbally exchange minimal information with another person, either on request
or spontaneously.

> EXAMPLES
>   1. answers a question about what he/she did over the weekend
>   2. talks about favorite sports team
>   3. talks about a TV program

303. respond appropriately with words to greetings and farewells.

> EXAMPLES
>   1. says "Hello," "Hi," or "Good morning" when greeted
>   2. responds verbally to "Good afternoon" with the same or similar farewell

304. ask appropriately for materials.

EXAMPLES
1. uses "Please" or "May I" to request items
2. waits for an appropriate time to request items
3. makes requests without yelling or demanding

305. verbally recall group rules and/or give reasons for rules, when requested by an adult.

EXAMPLES
1. explains rules for walking in the hall and reasons
2. explains lunchroom rules and reasons
3. explains student lounge/recreation rules and reasons
4. explains bus rules and reasons
5. explains rules for timeout area/room and reasons
6. explains rules regarding smoking and reasons
7. explains rules for earning and spending points along with reasons

306. speak using a volume appropriate for the situation.

EXAMPLES
1. speaks loud enough in group discussion for all to hear
2. speaks softly one-to-one so as not to disrupt others

307. wait, when expected, to be acknowledged verbally or by gesture before speaking.

EXAMPLES
1. remains quiet in group discussions until asked or given permission to speak
2. raises hand to indicate a desire to speak and waits until called on or given a gesture indicating permission

308. speak clearly.
(Note: If the student has an assessed speech disorder, see clinician for additional related objectives)

EXAMPLE
1. speaks at a rate with sufficient articulation that the listener can understand the message

309. wait until a speaker is finished before responding.

EXAMPLE
1. waits for a pause in conversations before beginning to speak

310. demonstrate listening by maintaining eye contact or by being able to summarize what was said.

> EXAMPLES
> 1. looks at the speaker when being spoken to
> 2. when asked, reiterates or summarizes the message

311. pause and allow others to speak.

> EXAMPLES
> 1. contributes thought in a discussion and then stops to allow others to speak
> 2. asks or encourages others to speak

312. initiate or pursue topics in conversations that are consistent or appropriate in the place, role, or social situation, given adult structure.

> EXAMPLES
> 1. at recess, in recreation areas, or during lunch, pursues conversation topics that do not offend others
> 2. refrains from initiating conversations on topics that take himself/herself or the group off task

313. participate minimally in discussions with relevant remarks, when given direct requests for a response.

> EXAMPLES
> 1. during social studies, responds to questions or volunteers answers related to the discussion
> 2. makes appropriate statements to group members in a class meeting

314. cease verbalizing, when directed by an adult.

> EXAMPLE
> 1. quits talking when asked by an adult

315. stay on the topic of discussion until it is appropriate to change or the discussion is ended.

> EXAMPLES
> 1. continues participation until class period ends
> 2. contributes to social group conversation without trying to change the topic others are interested in discussing

316. accept feedback from an adult about behavior or performance by allowing an adult to state observations.

EXAMPLES
1. listens to statements made by adults about his/her behavior without denials or projections
2. listens to an adult's comments while his/her point sheet is being marked
3. listens to an adult's comments while correcting assignment

317. accurately recall events when they are over.
(Note: Similar to Personal 314, except not in a counseling context.)

EXAMPLE
1. describes an event in a way that matches descriptions of others and/or is verifiable

318. respond appropriately to requests and directions from adults–prompts may be used.

EXAMPLES
1. when asked to begin, proceeds directly to start task
2. when asked to line up to leave the room, proceeds to directed place in line without comment
3. when asked to clean up work area, stops working and begins cleaning the area
4. when directed to do gym exercises, starts on cue
5. when asked to return to seat, does so promptly

319. express feelings about self or others to an adult appropriately.
(Note: Similar to Personal 306, except not in a counseling context.)

EXAMPLES
1. speaks privately to an adult about another student's behavior that bothers him/her
2. expresses pride or pleasure about skills in a class
3. privately expresses fears or worries
4. describes good feelings about a classmate's accomplishment

320. perform routine behavior described by verbal instructions, given directly to him/her by an adult, without reminders or additional cues.

EXAMPLES
1. given direction, returns promptly to seat and sits down
2. puts materials away at the end of class when directed
3. begins clean-up when directed at the end of cooking class
4. gets out necessary materials for class when directed
5. returns signed field trip permission slip by due date

LEVEL 2 Long-Term Goals—Communication Behaviors

1. The student will use words to express oneself appropriately in group situations.
2. The student will use words and behaviors to contribute to group success.

Objectives: The student will...

221. initiate conversations with people in various classes or social situations, making oneself clear and understandable.

EXAMPLES
1. asks appropriate questions of a guest speaker
2. greets and talks with a visitor to the class
3. visits appropriately with staff in casual conversation

222. reply to conversational questions appropriately.

EXAMPLES
1. when asked about weekend activities, describes events that happened
2. responds to questions about personal interests

223. correctly follow verbal directions, when given to the group, without an individual prompt.

EXAMPLES
1. completes an assignment correctly following an explanation given to the class
2. takes assigned place in group following an adult direction
3. does the correct exercise following direction in gym
4. proceeds to assigned seat at a school assembly following direction to the group

224. attend when another student is speaking with permission.

EXAMPLES
1. looks at the student who is talking during a group discussion
2. refrains from talking to others while a designated student is speaking
3. refrains from playing with objects or making noise while another student is speaking

225. contribute to making group rules.

EXAMPLES
1. offers suggestion when the group is asked to decide on a game in gym
2. suggests reasonable consequences for violation of a class rule
3. offers suggestion for how the group should walk in the hall
4. offers suggestion for group behavior on a field trip

226. verbalize established consequences if group rules are broken.

EXAMPLE
1. correctly states specific consequence(s) for violation(s) when questioned by staff

227. spontaneously participate in group discussions.

EXAMPLES
1. contributes to social studies discussion without prompts
2. contributes to feedback or group session without prompts
3. joins in a social conversation during free time

228. verbally direct feeling of anger or distress at appropriate source–person, object, or situation.

EXAMPLES
1. speaks directly to a person causing him/her to feel angry
2. verbalizes frustration with a troublesome math task
3. verbalizes frustration with the computer
4. verbalizes distress to the teacher about a desired class not being available

229. verbally recognize feelings of others, either spontaneously or in response to questions.

EXAMPLES
1. describes parent's pleasure about a recent good grade
2. acknowledges a peer's pleasure about winning a ball game
3. acknowledges a peer's anger about being called a name
4. acknowledges an adult's frustration when the group is off task

230. maintain appropriate social distance when speaking to another.

EXAMPLES
1. for elementary students, respects personal space by standing 2 to 3 feet away from the other person(s)
2. for middle school and older students, respects personal space by standing 3 or more feet away from the other person(s)

231. verbally acknowledge another's strengths, achievements, or positive attributes with appropriate compliments.

EXAMPLES
1. compliments a student about participation in gym
2. congratulates a student on a promotion in the program
3. compliments a student on appearance
4. compliments a student for staying calm when another student was trying to provoke him/her
5. compliments a student about artistic skills

232. verbally acknowledge the effects of positive and negative language or behavior when directed at others.

EXAMPLES
1. explains how another student will respond to being teased
2. explains how another student will respond to compliments
3. explains how another student will respond to encouragement
4. explains likely response to request beginning with the word "please"

233. appropriately respond with words to positive or negative comments from others.

EXAMPLES
1. responds with "Thank you" when given a compliment
2. responds with "I don't like it when you talk to me that way" when teased
3. responds with "It makes me mad when you say _____"
4. responds with "I enjoy working with you" when thanked for help that has been given

234. tell peers more appropriate ways to behave in a given situation.

EXAMPLES
1. offers a suggestion for how a peer could solve a problem with another student
2. asks a student to remain calm when being provoked
3. tells a student to try again when frustrated and ready to quit a task
4. tells a student to be more respectful to the substitute teacher
5. offers a suggestion to the group about how to support a group member who is having a problem

LEVEL 1 Long-Term Goals—Communication Behaviors

1. The student will use words to establish and/or enrich social relationships, independent of adult structure.
2. The student will demonstrate ability to appropriately express personal opinions and needs and to recognize those communicated by others.

Objectives: The student will...

135. initiate appropriate greetings and farewells toward others.

> EXAMPLES
> 1. says "Good morning" before being greeted by another
> 2. says "Have a nice evening" when leaving school

136. speak courteously to others, using appropriate references, with no cues.

> EXAMPLES
> 1. says "Mr., Mrs., Miss, or Ms._____" when addressing an adult
> 2. says "Excuse me" when attempting to walk around a group of people

137. express personal opinion appropriately to adults and/or peers about new task or activity in which success is, or may be, questionable.

> EXAMPLES
> 1. explains why he/she does not want to do a task
> 2. tells the teacher that he/she is afraid to do a task
> 3. tells the teacher that he/she doesn't know how to do a new task

138. verbalize desire and plans for returning to, or participating in, the mainstream classes or other less restrictive educational programs.

> EXAMPLES
> 1. tells the teacher or counselor that he/she would like to begin the process to take regular classes
> 2. participates in discussion to plan for transition to class(es) in another program

139. respond appropriately to the actions of others as social cues.

> EXAMPLES
> 1. smiles in response to a smile from the teacher
> 2. reaches out to shake hands when offered by another
> 3. quits talking in response to a nonverbal gesture
> 4. takes place in line at water fountain without direction

140. verbally redirect peers on task when appropriate.

EXAMPLES
1. politely tells a peer to help with a group art project
2. politely asks a peer to be quiet while rules are being explained for a new game in gym
3. tells a peer to stop fooling around and help with assignment
4. politely tells a peer to stop talking or making noise because it is distracting
5. as team captain for a game, reminds players of their roles

141. verbalize positive feelings and expectations about self.

EXAMPLES
1. tells the teacher "I did a really good job in math today"
2. tells a peer "I can solve this (problem) by myself"
3. tells the social worker "I had a very good day, will you call my mother and tell her?"
4. tells the teacher "I will pass this test"
5. tells the teacher "I am going to try to get an A"
6. writes a goal to get promoted to a new program or school

142. praise and personally support others, without adult prompts.

EXAMPLES
1. tells teammates when they do a good job in a ball game
2. tells a teammate to "Shake it off" after a poor play
3. encourages a peer not to give up on a difficult task
4. recognizes when a peer is upset and says "Is there anything I can do to help?"
5. congratulates a peer on getting a good grade
6. wishes a peer well when the peer is leaving the program

143. verbally demonstrate knowledge of the limits and expectations of the mainstream schools.

EXAMPLES
1. correctly explains/describes the level of work completion that may be expected in a same-grade regular class
2. correctly describes behavioral rules and consequences

144. describe personal strengths that will enable success in mainstream classes.

EXAMPLES
1. says "I know how and where to get help when I need it"
2. says "I am good at reading and know how to follow written directions"
3. says "I can do well with a work-study program and classes 'a', 'b', and 'c'"
4. says "I will finish assignments, including homework"

Interpersonal Behaviors

DEFINITION

The student demonstrates the skills that enable him/her
to interact with others in social and task situations in
ways that meet personal and interdependent needs
and that contribute to a sense of belonging.

LEVEL 3 Long-Term Goals—Interpersonal Behaviors

1. The student will participate in selected adult-structured activities
   with other students.
2. The student will demonstrate knowledge of and compliance
   with basic social rules for constructive interactions.

Objectives: The student will...

301. be aware of and attend to adult behavior (appropriate behavior not required).

> EXAMPLES
> 1. looks in the direction of the adult
> 2. looks away from the adult
> 3. responds in any way to the adult's movement or verbalization

302. respond to an adult when his/her name is called.

> EXAMPLES
> 1. looks at the adult when his/her name is called
> 2. verbally responds when his/her name is called

303. engage in organized solitary entertainment, with directions from an adult.

> EXAMPLES
> 1. works with a puzzle provided by the adult
> 2. listens to an audiotape provided by the teacher
> 3. draws or paints a picture with materials provided
> 4. plays a game on the computer

304. participate in sharing activity when verbally directed by an adult.

> EXAMPLES
> 1. shares art materials provided for use on individual work
> 2. shares basketball with others during open shooting time
> 3. shares cookies or candy with peers
> 4. shares time on the computer

305. respond appropriately, when requested, to come to an adult in non-crisis situations.

> EXAMPLE
> 1. walks promptly up to the adult when asked

306. respond appropriately to social interactions initiated by another student.

> EXAMPLES
> 1. joins in a group game when invited by a peer
> 2. joins in casual conversation when addressed by a peer
> 3. responds to a peer's questions about interests
> 4. responds to greetings and farewells initiated by a peer

307. approach another student with a verbal or physical gesture of friendship.

> EXAMPLES
> 1. initiates a greeting
> 2. invites a peer to join in a game
> 3. offers to share treats with a peer
> 4. offers to help a peer with math problem
> 5. offers a compliment to start a conversation

308. accept help from an adult, when offered, on routine non-academic tasks or activities.

> EXAMPLES
> 1. accepts advice on how to decide teams for gym class
> 2. accepts advice on how to decide among art project choices
> 3. accepts help with adding up points earned during the day
> 4. accepts advice on how to set a personal goal for the day

309. seek an adult to help on routine non-academic tasks or activities.

> EXAMPLES
> 1. asks an adult for assistance in finding materials for _____
> 2. asks an adult for a suggestion for a free-time activity
> 3. asks an adult for help getting a phone number

310. engage in parallel activities with another student working at the same table or in the same area.

EXAMPLES
1. works alone on an art project at the same table with peers
2. works alone on a math task at the same table with peers
3. works independently next to others in the computer lab
4. works independently next to others in shop class

311. seek adult attention appropriately by engaging in conversation or activity.

EXAMPLES
1. during recess, converses with an adult about a movie
2. during lunch, converses with an adult about music
3. asks an adult to play a table game during choice time
4. shares a story about a family activity with an adult
5. asks an adult to share a story about a topic of mutual interest

312. accept compliments and praise from adults and peers.

EXAMPLES
1. smiles or says "Thank you" when complimented on clothes
2. smiles or says "Thank you" when complimented on a success or special effort
3. acknowledges a compliment by returning it with a compliment

313. play simple competitive games according to rules.

EXAMPLES
1. plays table games according to the rules
2. plays table tennis according to the rules
3. plays kickball according to the rules

314. minimally participate in adult-structured, group non-academic activities, with prompts or encouragement.

EXAMPLES
1. reluctantly plays basketball when all other players are opposite sex
2. sits in music class, but sings only when prompted
3. works sluggishly on an art project he/she doesn't want to do
4. participates in role plays during social skills training

315. sit quietly for 15 minutes or more in a group listening activity.

EXAMPLES
1. listens while an adult is reading a story
2. listens while a visiting adult is making a presentation
3. listens to a presentation during a school assembly

316. respond appropriately to adult intervention during a group problem or crisis by following directions given to him/her.

EXAMPLES
1. remains quietly seated, when directed, as an adult intervenes
2. goes to get help when directed by an adult
3. moves to another area in the room when directed

317. allow interpersonal interactions between others (students and adults) without attempting to control them.

EXAMPLES
1. waits to be invited before interrupting a game or a conversation
2. asks permission appropriately to join an activity or a conversation
3. refrains from commenting or making gestures that may interfere with or provoke others

318. refrain from initiating or encouraging conflicts between others.

EXAMPLES
1. limits comments to, or about, others to statements that are courteous, complimentary, or otherwise nonprovocative
2. refrains from verbal and nonverbal gestures that may reinforce or escalate an existing conflict between peers
3. refrains from making comments or nonverbal gestures when a peer is being confronted or given direction by an adult

---

LEVEL 2 Long-Term Goals—Interpersonal Behaviors

1. The student will participate in and contribute to the success of interdependent activities focused on collective group goals.
2. The student will demonstrate knowledge of individuals' differences and how individuals' behaviors contribute to or interfere with personal and group success.

Objectives: The student will...

219. refrain from initiating conflict with others.

EXAMPLES
1. speaks courteously to others, using "Please" and "Thank you" when making requests
2. addresses peers by their given names or accepted nicknames
3. does not draw, present, or gesture in symbols that are associated with street gangs
4. avoids use of nonverbal gestures that are provocative

220. participate in peer group activities when asked by peers.

EXAMPLES
1. joins in a game when asked
2. joins a group conversation when asked

221. participate in cooperative activities on projects structured by an adult.

EXAMPLES
1. helps prepare food for class party
2. joins a group to help plan a class event
3. helps a group paint a class mural
4. takes a part in a class skit

222. take turns, without verbal reminders by an adult.

EXAMPLES
1. spontaneously takes a place in line for lunch
2. spontaneously shares the basketball during recess
3. volunteers to let a peer be first in a game

223. suggest activities or preference for group recreation to an adult.

EXAMPLES
1. when asked, suggests that the group play kickball in gym
2. when asked, suggests a table game
3. when asked, suggests a movie for earned group time

224. develop positive relationships with more than one adult.

EXAMPLES
1. visits comfortably with different adults at lunch
2. asks to show an assignment with an "A" to another adult
3. welcomes staff from other classes into the room
4. accepts advice or help from staff other than his/her favorite adult

225. share materials and equipment, with minimal reminders from an adult.

EXAMPLES
1. when the allotted time is up on the computer, invites the next student to take his/her turn
2. shares colored pens with a peer working on personal projects
3. passes a tool in shop class to a peer when finished
4. passes a magazine to a peer when finished

226. conform to group decisions and participate despite disappointment or disagreement.

EXAMPLES
1. participates in gym game, suggested by peer, that he/she did not want to do
2. participates in a field trip that is different from the one he/she suggested
3. plays checkers when he/she wanted to play chess

227. display developing friendships by showing preference for a specific student or group.

EXAMPLES
1. routinely asks to work with the same student(s) on cooperative learning tasks
2. chooses the same student(s) to play games with during free time
3. sits by the same student(s) during lunch

228. recognize and describe individual differences of others.

EXAMPLES
1. describes a peer as polite and fair
2. describes a peer as friendly and nice
3. describes a peer as mean
4. describes a peer as smart

229. accept and adhere to game rules, without reminders from an adult.

EXAMPLES
1. plays games without cheating
2. takes turn in proper order

230. accept constructive criticism from an adult.

EXAMPLES
1. agrees to include a student who was left out by the group
2. acknowledges an adult's concern and apologizes for being inconsiderate to a peer or adult
3. modifies behavior when being confronted about being too aggressive in a basketball game
4. slows to a walk when reminded that running in the hall may hurt someone

231. accept new participants into an on-going activity.

EXAMPLES
1. invites a peer to be on his/her team in the game
2. asks a peer to join the group working on a project
3. agrees to reorganize teams to accommodate a new player

232. suggest an appropriate activity for the group directly to peers, without adult direction.

EXAMPLES
1. suggests going outside for gym because of nice weather
2. suggests requesting permission for a celebration party
3. suggests making a card for a classmate or staff member who is ill
4. suggests a tournament with another class or school

233. accept and respond appropriately to positive peer pressure.

EXAMPLES
1. ceases inconsiderate comments when confronted by peers
2. stops making noises when confronted by peers
3. refrains from truanting class when confronted by peers

234. participate in group planning and constructive problem solving, with adult structure.

EXAMPLES
1. participates in group discussion about how to help a peer who has been suspended for a behavioral violation
2. participates in group discussion about how to resolve a fight in the lunch room
3. participates in group discussion about solving the problem of someone in the group stealing things
4. participates in group discussion about how the group will decide activities the group will do during choice time

LEVEL 1 Long-Term Goals—Interpersonal Behaviors

1. The student will spontaneously participate in group tasks and social activities.
2. The student will initiate and maintain positive relationships, independent of adult structure.

Objectives: The student will...

135. participate in difficult games requiring skills, scoring, and knowledge of rules.

EXAMPLES
1. learns and plays chess by the rules
2. learns and plays Monopoly by the rules

136. spontaneously participate in peer group activities.

EXAMPLES
1. asks to be included in a game
2. joins with peers in deciding and beginning a game
3. joins in friendly conversation during lunch or recess
4. joins the group to help finish a bulletin board
5. joins in helping the group clean up after pizza party

137. disapprove of offensive peer behavior by ignoring or actively discouraging it.

EXAMPLES
1. ignores a peer's inappropriate attention-seeking behavior
2. appropriately confronts a peer about teasing a classmate
3. asks a classmate to stop swearing
4. politely asks a classmate to stop making a disruptive noise
5. politely asks peers to be quiet so the class can line up for lunch

138. verbally indicate preferences among group members by differentiating personal characteristics/behaviors.

EXAMPLES
1. explains that he/she prefers to work with a specific peer because he/she does not fool around
2. explains that he/she wants a specific peer on the spelling team because he/she is smart
3. explains that he/she wants a specific peer on the baseball team because he/she is a good athlete
4. explains that he/she wants to work with a specific peer on the art task because he/she shares
5. explains that he/she likes to play checkers with a specific peer because he/she does not cheat

139. physically or verbally come to the support of another student by offering assistance in a difficult situation.

EXAMPLES
1. calmly consoles an angry classmate who has been teased
2. comforts a classmate who has just been injured
3. offers a helpful suggestion to a peer about a problem at home
4. offers to help a peer who is frustrated with an assignment

140. participate in group planning, problem solving, or decision making, with minimal adult participation.
(Note: Similar to Personal 234, except without adult-imposed structure.)

EXAMPLE
1. participates in a peer mediation session when offered

141. spontaneously demonstrate positive leadership behaviors.

EXAMPLES
1. begins cleaning up after a project without a direction
2. initiates suggestions for activities
3. initiates behaviors to welcome new classmate
4. follows school/class behavioral expectations without cues
5. invites others to join in activities
6. suggests and helps in ways to organize a group activity
7. is patient with followers
8. encourages others who are having difficulty

142. spontaneously resist negative peer pressure.

EXAMPLES
1. refuses to follow a friend's suggestion to run from or skip class
2. refuses offer of a cigarette
3. refuses to join in the teasing or harassment of a peer
4. tells an adult about how he/she was able to resist drinking or other prohibited behaviors outside of school

Task Behaviors

DEFINITION

The student engages in learning tasks and activities that are routinely assigned by the teacher and for which grades or credits are received. These behaviors include preparing for a learning activity, attempting assignments, and demonstrating growth.

LEVEL 3 Long-Term Goals—Task Behaviors

1. The student will attempt assigned individualized tasks.
2. The student will accept and seek adult assistance.
3. The student will minimally participate in group tasks.

Objectives: The student will...

301. attempt individualized academic tasks assigned, with assistance if needed or provided.

> EXAMPLES
> 1. begins a math problem with adult attention
> 2. answers a worksheet question with adult support
> 3. reads directions and begins task
> 4. begins a task following specific instruction

302. accept assistance from an adult on academic tasks.

> EXAMPLES
> 1. resumes work on a task when an adult provides help
> 2. thanks an adult for the help provided

303. demonstrate short-term memory for directions by proceeding on task without reminders.

> EXAMPLES
> 1. completes similar type adding problems after receiving help
> 2. completes one step in a shop project after explanation
> 3. completes a worksheet on CVC vowel pattern after explanation
> 4. completes a worksheet on capitalization after explanation

304. agree to and complete academic testing.

> EXAMPLES
> 1. takes and makes a reasonable effort on standardized tests
> 2. takes reading, spelling, math, or other subject quizzes
> 3. takes Curriculum Based Measurement timings

305. appropriately seek assistance from an adult on academic tasks.

> EXAMPLES
> 1. makes some effort to solve a problem before asking for help
> 2. raises hand or in other acceptable manner requests help
> 3. continues work on a task after help has been provided

306. minimally participate in group-focused classes that are required.

> EXAMPLES
> 1. watches and listens to the discussion
> 2. does not distract others with off-task behaviors
> 3. responds to questions when called on

307. respond appropriately to instructions given by an adult for beginning and/or completing an assignment. *and or asking for help if needed.*

> EXAMPLES
> 1. takes an assignment handed out by the teacher and begins work
> 2. turns in an assignment when requested

308. watch audiovisual presentations.

> EXAMPLE
> 1. is awake and attending to the movie or slide presentation

309. refrain from inappropriate behavior when asked by an adult to correct errors on academic tasks.

> EXAMPLES
> 1. makes corrections on math problems without complaining
> 2. makes corrections on a spelling assignment without destroying the worksheet
> 3. asks for an explanation

310. participate in physical education class.

> EXAMPLE
> 1. engages in the expected activities, following instruction from the teacher

311. complete daily reading/English assignment.

EXAMPLES
1. works consistently on task for the full class time allotted or until the task is completed
2. finishes the assignment and turns it in to the teacher

312. complete daily math assignment.

EXAMPLES
1. works consistently on task for the full class time allotted or until the task is completed
2. finishes the assignment and turns it in to the teacher

313. work independently for 10 to 20 minutes on assigned tasks.

SELF-EXPLANATORY

314. attempt to verbally answer questions when called on in group-structured classes.

EXAMPLES
1. responds with the answer or best guess
2. explains that he/she doesn't know an answer if he/she doesn't

---

LEVEL 2 Long-Term Goals—Task Behaviors

1. The student will routinely participate in group-structured academic tasks.
2. The student will follow written instructions for academic assignments.
3. The student will accept instruction and follow directions from different teachers for different classes.

Objectives: The student will...

215. accept assistance from an adult on group academic tasks.

EXAMPLE
1. resumes a task as instructed with group members present

216. share materials or take turns when directed during group tasks.

EXAMPLES
1. shares the calculator in math class
2. shares the dictionary in English class
3. shares the maps in social studies class
4. shares the equipment in science class
5. brings an object in for "show-and-tell time"

217. volunteer appropriate answers to questions in group discussions.

EXAMPLES
1. raises hand to be called on when he/she knows the correct answer to a question
2. offers an opinion when a question does not have one correct answer

218. participate in team activities during physical education classes.

EXAMPLE
1. takes place on team and participates without personal cue from an adult

219. actively participate in mini-classes or other special-focus classes.

EXAMPLES
1. attends to discussion and contributes in sex education class
2. attends to discussion and contributes in social skills class

220. choose and actively participate in elective classes.

EXAMPLES
1. asks questions about available classes and makes choices
2. responds to directions and participates in the required activities of the selected classes

221. work independently for periods of 20 to 30 minutes.

SELF-EXPLANATORY

222. ignore the routine distractions of others while doing seat work.

EXAMPLES
1. continues on task while others ask for and receive help
2. continues on task while a visitor enters the room to talk with the teacher

223. given directions by an adult, correct own work and turn in completed assignments.

    EXAMPLES
1. reviews a math assignment returned with errors noted, makes appropriate corrections, and turns it in again
2. corrects spelling and punctuation errors on an English assignment and turns it in

224. when finished with an assignment, select an activity from choices provided to occupy oneself for the remainder of the class period.

    EXAMPLES
1. when finished with an assignment, works on a drawing
2. when finished with an assignment, selects a magazine or book
3. when finished with an assignment, does catch-up work on another incomplete assignment

225. self-chart or log progress in reading and/or math.

    EXAMPLE
1. keeps a chart or other type of graph on progress

226. complete all assignments.
(Note: Should result in earning required grades or credits.)

    SELF-EXPLANATORY

LEVEL 1 Long-Term Goals—Task Behaviors

1. The student will routinely work on and complete assignments in classes that simulate mainstream classrooms.
2. The student will be prepared and come to classes with appropriate materials.
3. The student will complete, with passing grades, at least 2 hours per day of mainstream classes.

Objectives: The student will...

127. participate in academic classes that simulate mainstream classes.

    EXAMPLE
1. spontaneously engages in routine daily academic activities and expectations that are organized to simulate a regular education classroom

128. use time productively while waiting for assistance, when needed.

> EXAMPLES
> 1. when stuck on a problem or question, works on other problems until the teacher is able to help
> 2. when stuck on a problem or question, rereads directions to try to figure out the solution

129. contribute to class discussions and activities by bringing in materials, relating personal experiences, suggesting ideas, or planning projects.

> EXAMPLES
> 1. brings in a relevant newspaper clipping to share with class
> 2. shares a personal story relevant to the discussion
> 3. suggests ideas for class play or music performance

130. participate in structured role-playing simulations of mainstream classroom situations.

> EXAMPLES
> 1. engages in role play of how to ask a teacher for directions in front of a large class
> 2. engages in role play of how to ask permission to see support staff or an administrator for help with a problem
> 3. engages in role play of how to ask a peer for help with an assignment
> 4. engages in role play of how to develop a plan for completing homework assignments
> 5. engages in role play of how to make friends in a new school

131. complete all assignments within the time they are due.

> SELF-EXPLANATORY

132. work independently for periods of 30 to 40 minutes.

> SELF-EXPLANATORY

133. take a test on an assignment following verbal and/or written directions.

> SELF-EXPLANATORY

134. seek and work independently on alternate or other academic tasks when assigned tasks are completed.
(Note: Similar to Task 224, except that available choices are academic.)

> SELF-EXPLANATORY

135. complete and turn in assigned homework when due.

> SELF-EXPLANATORY

Personal Behaviors

DEFINITION

The student engages in dialog with a counseling adult, permitting the adult to assist the student in resolving personal issues, developing personal skills, and building a sense of self-worth.

Note: "Counselor" in this document refers to an adult who is in the role, or circumstance, of providing services relating to the following objectives. This person may be a social worker, psychologist, special education teacher, or other trained adult.

LEVEL 3 Long-Term Goals—Personal Behaviors

1. The student will attend to and accept input/feedback from an adult.
2. The student will demonstrate a developing trust with selected adults by responding appropriately to help that is offered.
3. The student will accurately label personal feelings to an adult.

Objectives: The student will...

301. attend sessions under duress, when directed or offered by an adult.

EXAMPLES
1. complains, but complies with direction to meet with the "counselor"
2. accompanies the "counselor" to the office when suggested

302. demonstrate attention to the adult speaking by maintaining eye contact or restating information.

EXAMPLES
1. restates information, stated by the adult, in his/her own words
2. looks at the adult who is speaking
3. nods head or engages in other nonverbal responses to acknowledge statements by the adult

303. participate verbally in sessions.

> EXAMPLES
> 1. verbally responds to questions with intelligible and appropriate language
> 2. asks appropriate questions
> 3. verbally explains or acknowledges the reason for the session

304. accept positive feedback from an adult about behavior.

> EXAMPLES
> 1. says "Thank you" or demonstrates acceptance of praise
> 2. smiles when praised for a specific behavior

305. express negative feelings to an adult.

> EXAMPLES
> 1. yells or bursts out about an incident
> 2. complains about another student
> 3. complains about an adult
> 4. complains about a situation
> 5. cries

306. verbally acknowledge and describe personal feelings in one-to-one situation with an adult.

> EXAMPLES
> 1. agrees when the adult says "You are very angry"
> 2. agrees when the adult says "You look very sad"
> 3. says "I get frightened when _____"
> 4. says "I really like it when _____"
> 5. says "I get angry when _____"
> 6. says "I don't want my mother mad at me"

307. accept feedback from an adult about his/her feelings.

> EXAMPLES
> 1. listens to the adult say "It is OK to be upset"
> 2. begins to cry when the adult says "You are very sad"
> 3. admits being angry when his/her behavior is interpreted
> 4. admits being frightened
> 5. admits that "I don't care" statement is a cover-up

308. follow through with specific directions from an adult to modify behavior in a given situation.

EXAMPLES
1. when returned to class, complies with specific instructions about what to say to a peer
2. when returned to class, complies with specific instructions about what to say to an to adult
3. when returned to class, complies with instruction to restore disturbed area
4. when returned to class, complies with instruction to begin task

309. initiate verbal interaction by requesting counseling assistance.

EXAMPLES
1. when feeling angry or frustrated, appropriately requests permission to talk about the problem with an adult
2. when needing help to make an appointment with another agency, asks permission to see the "counselor"
3. when concerned about a problem at home, asks to see the "counselor"

310. remain seated in appropriate place during counseling sessions.

EXAMPLE
1. while in a session with the "counselor," remains in the chair provided until the meeting is complete

311. listen to alternatives for resolving a problem and choose one.

EXAMPLES
1. restates in his/her own words alternatives presented for solving a problem and states which one he/she will try
2. asks questions about the implications of alternatives presented before stating which one he/she will try

312. verbalize that he/she has friends.

EXAMPLES
1. gives the name(s) of person(s) considered a friend(s)
2. describes relationship with a person considered a friend

313. verbalize understanding of logical consequences of behavior.

EXAMPLES
1. explains that if you miss lunch, you will be hungry
2. explains that if you do not follow your mother's directions, she will be angry
3. explains that if you stay up late at night, you will be tired in school
4. explains that if you do a good job on your assignments, you will get a good grade
5. explains that if you don't look where you are running, you could get hurt
6. explains that if you don't graduate from school, it will be hard to get a good job
7. explains that if you tease others, they will get angry with you

314. accurately recall events when they are over.

EXAMPLES
1. describes an event in a way that matches descriptions of others and/or is verifiable
2. tells the truth

315. verbally initiate positive interactions with an adult.

EXAMPLES
1. asks to show an adult a good grade on an assignment
2. asks to show an adult a good point sheet
3. initiates conversation about a pleasurable event
4. says "Thank you" for something an adult did for him/her
5. compliments an adult
6. asks an adult to help with, or comment on, a positive personal goal
7. asks to spend some "fun" time with a favored adult

316. remain on counseling task/topic for the duration of the session.

EXAMPLES
1. refrains from diverting discussion to off-task topic
2. responds to questions and comments from the adult

317. participate in determining a short-term plan for dealing with an immediate situation.

EXAMPLE
1. asks questions and offers opinions about possible solution for dealing with a problem when returning to class or for the remainder of the day

318. negotiate and successfully complete terms of daily contracts.

EXAMPLE
1. discusses, agrees to, and meets the terms of a contract for one day at a time

319. react to situations with appropriate emotional response–pleasure, anger, fear, or sadness.

EXAMPLE
1. demonstrates an appropriate match between expressed feelings and an event or circumstance, such as smiling when complimented, crying when teased, or yelling when angry

320. verbalize feelings about self to an adult.

EXAMPLES
1. says "I feel good about myself"
2. says "I am angry with myself"
3. says "I know I can do better"
4. says "I feel dumb"
5. says "I am good at _____ , but not so good at _____"
6. says "I really wish that I _____"

321. verbalize the fact of consequences for own behavior.

EXAMPLES
1. says "I am tired because I stayed up late"
2. says "I went to timeout because _____"
3. says "I failed because I did not do the work"
4. says "I got an 'A' because I worked hard"
5. says "I am off probation because I changed my behavior"
6. says "I missed recess because I did not finish my work"
7. says "I had a good day because I followed directions"

LEVEL 2 Long-Term Goals—Personal Behaviors

1. The student will verbally demonstrate knowledge of the relationship among feelings, behaviors, and consequences.
2. The student will verbally demonstrate knowledge or ability to clarify personal expectations of others.
3. The student will verbally demonstrate ability to identify or describe the feelings of others.

Objectives: The student will...

222. verbally describe characteristics of friendships.

EXAMPLES
1. says "Friends don't lie to you"
2. says "Friends are fair with you"
3. says "Friends don't steal things from you"
4. says "Friends treat you nice"

223. verbally acknowledge misdirected anger, but may or may not follow with corrective behavior.

EXAMPLES
1. admits that it was really a student, not the teacher, who made him/her angry
2. apologizes for yelling at the teacher when it was something else that he/she was angry about

224. attend to a peer when peer is speaking.

EXAMPLES
1. looks at a peer or paraphrases a peer's comment in group session
2. refrains from interrupting or other distracting behaviors in group session

225. appropriately accept positive feedback from peers.

EXAMPLES
1. smiles or says "Thank you" when complimented by a peer
2. when complimented, smiles and responds with a compliment

226. provide peers with appropriate feedback, within an adult-provided structure.

EXAMPLES
1. in group session, tells a peer that he/she enjoyed working with him/her on _____
2. in group session, tells a peer that he/she did a good job of dealing with the problem with _____
3. in group session, tells a peer that he/she did not like it when he/she did _____
4. in group session, reminds a peer that he/she is responsible for his/her own behavior
5. in group session, confronts a peer about how the rest of the class was penalized because of his/her behavior

227. accept designated leadership role in group.

EXAMPLES
1. when given the role, takes the group through a guided session
2. when given the role, reinforces the members who follow group procedures and confronts members who do not

228. express feelings about self to peers.

EXAMPLES
1. tells the group about a personal accomplishment that day and that he/she feels really good about it
2. tells the group about a problem and that he/she feels disappointed
3. tells the group about an issue and that he/she feels angry

229. verbalize desire to successfully return to regular or less restrictive school or program.

EXAMPLES
1. talks about wanting to go to a different school and what he/she will need to do to be successful there
2. talks about how current growth and achievement will help him/her be successful in regular classes

230. seek counseling to avoid conflict.

EXAMPLE
1. requests to see an adult for help when angry, frustrated, or anxious about a problem before trying to handle it alone

231. attend counseling, when directed by an adult, without objections.

EXAMPLE
1. willingly meets with an adult for counseling when directed to deal with a current problem

232. participate in compromise.

> EXAMPLES
> 1. suggests taking turns as a solution to a group member wanting different activities
> 2. listens to others' suggestions and negotiates agreement
> 3. follows through when compromise is agreed to

233. participate in the development of a personal plan for a period of one to six weeks, with help from others.

> EXAMPLES
> 1. listens to alternatives, asks questions, offers opinions, and agrees to a plan for self-management for at least one week
> 2. negotiates a behavioral contract and agrees to its terms for at least one week

234. verbally describe situations accurately that distress him/her and/or lead to a crisis.

> EXAMPLES
> 1. explains behavior(s) of a peer that makes him/her feel angry
> 2. explains behavior(s) of an adult that makes him/her feel angry
> 3. explains nature of assignment(s) that makes him/her feel frustrated
> 4. explains events at home that make him/her feel upset

235. verbally demonstrate understanding that personal frustration and stress are normal.

> EXAMPLES
> 1. gives examples of circumstances where people typically get frustrated, e.g., not getting what you want
> 2. accurately describes common events or situations that are frustrating and gives examples of how he/she appropriately manages the stress

236. participate in developing a short-term plan for the group for a 2-week period.

> EXAMPLES
> 1. helps the group set an attendance goal so all can go on a field trip
> 2. helps the group set a work-completion goal so all can _____
> 3. helps the group decide on a plan for dealing with a problem with a group member

237. verbally demonstrate willingness to accept not getting his/her own way by acknowledging the fact and conforming to a decision.

> EXAMPLE
> 1. agrees that it is not fair to always get what he/she wants and readily participates in the desired activity of other group members

LEVEL 1 Long-Term Goals—Personal Behaviors

1. The student will compare different values and clarify personal priorities.
2. The student will develop realistic personal expectations.
3. The student will assert personal needs and feelings while respecting the rights of others.

Objectives: The student will...

138. use verbal and nonverbal behaviors to express pride.

EXAMPLES
1. asks to take an art project home
2. asks to take an English paper home
3. asks to show achievement to the administrator
4. asks parent to come to awards day ceremony
5. asks if a friend can visit the school
6. takes achievement award home
7. asks for extra time to work on a shop project
8. asks if someone at school would give a job reference

139. list and compare consequences of own behaviors in different situations.

EXAMPLES
1. gives accurate description of how he/she handled a conflict with a peer and what happened
2. describes an event in which an adult mistakenly accused him/her of misconduct and how different ways of responding have different outcomes
3. describes how he/she handles problems at home compared to school and explains why
4. explains potentially different consequences for getting angry and losing control at school compared with at a job

140. contribute to group rule making and consequences.

EXAMPLES
1. helps the group decide rules for lunchroom behavior so class can have the privilege of _____
2. helps the group decide goal for completing assignments so class can have the privilege of _____
3. helps the group decide rules for time on the computer so all get a fair opportunity

141. participate in a group plan for a period of 2 to 5 weeks.
(Note: Similar to Personal 236, except longer in duration.)

SELF-EXPLANATORY

142. initiate goal setting for self.

EXAMPLES
1. without prompts, describes a specific achievable goal and asks for feedback
2. without prompts, describes a sequence of steps in a plan for success on a goal

143. initiate problem solving or compromise for self.

EXAMPLES
1. without prompts, uses problem-solving steps to develop a plan for dealing with a conflict with a peer
2. without prompts, discusses modifying a goal to be realistic
3. without prompts, tells an adult about a personal problem and what alternatives he/she has considered for handling it

144. initiate problem solving or compromise for a group problem.

EXAMPLE
1. without prompts, uses problem-solving steps to accurately describe the problem and suggest possible solutions

145. verbalize understanding of regular school characteristics, expectations, limits, options, etc.

EXAMPLES
1. accurately describes typical class sizes, expectations, privileges, and responsibilities
2. accurately describes the school discipline code and consequences for rule violations
3. discusses the need to accept and adjust to varying attributes of different teachers and other staff
4. discusses the need to accept and adjust to diverse attributes of students

146. verbally demonstrate knowledge of alternative coping strategies for managing stress.

EXAMPLES
1. explains when and how to ask for help
2. explains when and how to use deep breathing
3. explains when and how to just walk away from conflict
4. explains how to use problem-solving steps
5. explains how to try to see another's point of view

147. verbally support and praise others for appropriate behavior in the group, without cues from an adult.

> EXAMPLES
>   1. spontaneously congratulates or compliments a peer on good work
>   2. spontaneously encourages a peer who is struggling
>   3. spontaneously reassures a disappointed peer

148. discuss the value of relationships with others and the characteristics of those relationships.

> EXAMPLES
>   1. explains or gives examples of what others have done to help him/her and describes feelings about the relationships
>   2. explains or gives examples of what others have done to harm him/her and describes feelings about the relationships

149. initiate and maintain interpersonal and group relationships with adults and peers.

> EXAMPLES
>   1. spontaneously introduces self to peers and adults
>   2. continues positive relationships with individuals described as friends or as supportive
>   3. joins boys/girls club, sports team, or other prosocial group for recreational or social activities

APPENDIX

Rating Scale Guide

Current Performance Form

Baseline Recording Forms

Target Objective Functional Analysis Planning Worksheet

Functional Analysis Planning Worksheet Summary

Individual Intervention Plan Form

Daily Monitoring Record

Team Meeting Notes

School-Community Agency Coordinated Intervention Plan

Interagency Meeting Notes

Target Behavior Performance Charts

Behavioral Progress Report

Annual Progress Summary Form

Rating Scale Guide

This Rating Scale Guide and the following Current Performance Form can be used to establish the student's current level of performance on the objectives. The *Behavioral Objective Sequence* items should be read carefully and literally. The examples are provided to add clarity to the intent of the objectives and to minimize the need for interpretation. Before conducting a rating, it is best to read through the entire instrument to become familiar with the scope and sequence of the objectives (skills) contained within the 233 items. Ratings should be based on direct observations over a period of 2 or more weeks. Ratings may be completed independently by individuals knowledgeable about the student, or ratings may represent the consensus of a team of observers. The scale **IS** a measure of how **FREQUENTLY** the student performs the skills. It **IS NOT** a measure of whether or not the student knows how to perform the skills.

Given your knowledge of the student and best judgment, rate each item on the Current Performance Form as follows:

The student demonstrates this objective...

0 = No basis for a judgment, don't know, or does not apply

1 = Never or rarely true (less than 30% of the time or opportunities)

2 = Sometimes true (between 30% and 60% of the time or opportunities)

3 = Often true (between 60% and 90% of the time or opportunities)

4 = Always or almost always true (90% or greater of the time or opportunities) This objective is mastered.

Use the rating of "0" as little as possible and only when you have no basis for a judgment or when it clearly does not apply in your setting.

A comparison of independently completed ratings will provide an opportunity to examine the possible situational effects of different settings on the student's behavior as well as variances in observers' perceptions that may offer helpful information for decisions about placement and intervention plans.

Current Performance Form

Page 1 of 3

Student _____ Teacher/Case Manager _____ Date _____

Summary of: Baseline___ 6TH WK___ 12TH WK___ 18TH WK___ 24TH WK___ 30TH WK___ 36TH WK___

Termination_____ Other _____ Performance Level: 3___ 2___ 1___

Adaptive: Responds appropriately to routine and new expectations

_____	301	demonstrate awareness of events
_____	302	attend 75% of school days
_____	303	remember routine daily schedule
_____	304	comply with bus-riding rules
_____	305	arrive at school on time
_____	306	bring no disruptive materials
_____	307	use non-classroom areas appropriately
_____	308	attend class on time and remain
_____	309	remain in school for its duration
_____	310	attend non-academic activities
_____	311	participate in non-academic activities—70%
_____	312	respond to changes without outbursts
_____	313	arrive at school physically clean
_____	314	try again when faced with disappointment
_____	315	follow rules outside of school building
_____	316	attempt new tasks
_____	317	eat at reasonable pace and clean the area
_____	318	wear appropriate clothing
_____	319	attend school daily
_____	320	follow common-sense safety rules

•••

_____	221	spontaneously participate in classes
_____	222	spontaneously participate in non-academic activities
_____	223	walk through halls appropriately with pass
_____	224	change activities without outbursts
_____	225	self-select appropriate activities
_____	226	demonstrate table manners
_____	227	complete individual and/or group tasks
_____	228	return property promptly and in good condition

•••

_____	129	wait for rewards for days or weeks
_____	130	bring required material for assignment to class
_____	131	participate regularly in mainstream classes
_____	132	accept support from mainstream resources
_____	133	complete mainstream classes with passing grades
_____	Individual	_____

Self-Management: Responds with self-control and seeks to be successful

_____	301	respond independently to materials for amusement
_____	302	appear alert and able to focus attention
_____	303	bring no weapons to school
_____	304	use amusement materials appropriately
_____	305	wait for turn without physical intervention
_____	306	use and return equipment without abuse
_____	307	accept positive physical contact
_____	308	touch others in appropriate ways
_____	309	refrain from stealing
_____	310	respond when angry without hitting
_____	311	recognize and show regard for possessions
_____	312	accept verbal cue for removal from a situation
_____	313	respond when angry without abuse of property
_____	314	respond appropriately to substitute
_____	315	respond when angry without threats
_____	316	walk to timeout without being moved by an adult

•••

_____	217	work or play without disrupting others
_____	218	refrain from inappropriate behavior when others lose control
_____	219	respond to provocation with self-control
_____	220	respond when angry with self-removal
_____	221	accept adult help in a crisis
_____	222	fulfill classroom job responsibilities
_____	223	seek adult help in a crisis
_____	224	comply with procedures in group situations
_____	225	demonstrate problem solving with assistance

•••

_____	126	fulfill responsibilities with minimal supervision
_____	127	maintain self-control when faced with disappointment
_____	128	obey new authority figure
_____	129	use personal skills to solve problems
_____	130	demonstrate knowledge of and work toward future rewards
_____	Individual	_____

Student _____ Teacher/Case Manager _____ Date _____

Summary of: Baseline___ 6TH WK___ 12TH WK___ 18TH WK___ 24TH WK___ 30TH WK___ 36TH WK___

Termination_____ Other_____. Performance Level: 3___ 2___ 1___

Communication: Demonstrates appropriate verbal and nonverbal skills

_____	301	answer a request with meaningful words
_____	302	verbally exchange minimal information
_____	303	respond appropriately to greetings and farewells
_____	304	ask appropriately for materials
_____	305	verbally recall group rules and/or give reasons
_____	306	speak using an appropriate volume
_____	307	wait to be acknowledged before speaking
_____	308	speak clearly
_____	309	wait until speaker is finished before responding
_____	310	demonstrate listening by eye contact or summarizing
_____	311	pause and allow others to speak
_____	312	initiate or pursue appropriate conversation topics
_____	313	participate minimally in discussion
_____	314	cease verbalizing when directed
_____	315	stay on topic
_____	316	accept feedback
_____	317	accurately recall events
_____	318	respond appropriately to requests
_____	319	express feelings
_____	320	perform routine behavior with verbal instructions

•••

_____	221	initiate conversations, making self understandable
_____	222	reply to conversational questions appropriately
_____	223	follow verbal directions given to the group
_____	224	attend when another student is speaking
_____	225	contribute to making group rules
_____	226	verbalize consequences for breaking group rules
_____	227	spontaneously participate in group discussions
_____	228	verbally direct feelings of anger at appropriate source
_____	229	verbally recognize feelings of others
_____	230	maintain appropriate distance when speaking to others
_____	231	verbally acknowledge another with appropriate compliments
_____	232	verbally acknowledge effects of positive and negative behavior
_____	233	appropriately respond with words to positive or negative comments
_____	234	tell peers more appropriate ways to behave

•••

_____	135	initiate appropriate greetings and farewells
_____	136	speak courteously to others, with no cues
_____	137	express personal opinions appropriately
_____	138	verbalize desire to return to mainstream classes
_____	139	respond appropriately to the actions of others
_____	140	verbally redirect peers on task
_____	141	verbalize positive feelings and self-expectations
_____	142	praise and support others, without prompts
_____	143	verbally demonstrate knowledge of mainstream schools
_____	144	describe strengths that will enable success in mainstream classes
_____	Individual	_____

Interpersonal: Interacts appropriately with others in social and task situations

_____	301	be aware of and attend to adult behavior
_____	302	respond to an adult when name is called
_____	303	engage in solitary entertainment
_____	304	participate in sharing activity
_____	305	respond appropriately to adult in non-crisis situations
_____	306	respond appropriately to social interactions
_____	307	approach another student with gesture of friendship
_____	308	accept help from an adult
_____	309	seek help from an adult
_____	310	engage in parallel activities with another student
_____	311	seek adult attention appropriately
_____	312	accept compliments and praise
_____	313	play games according to rules
_____	314	minimally participate in non-academic activities
_____	315	sit quietly for 15 minutes in group listening activity
_____	316	respond to a crisis by following directions
_____	317	allow interactions between others
_____	318	refrain from encouraging conflicts between others

•••

_____	219	refrain from initiating conflict with others
_____	220	participate in peer group activities
_____	221	participate in cooperative activities on projects
_____	222	take turns without verbal reminders
_____	223	suggest preference for group recreation
_____	224	develop positive relationships with more than one adult
_____	225	share materials, with minimal reminders
_____	226	conform to and participate in group decisions
_____	227	display developing friendships by showing preference
_____	228	recognize and describe individuals' differences
_____	229	accept and adhere to game rules
_____	230	accept criticism from an adult
_____	231	accept new participants in an activity
_____	232	suggest appropriate group activity
_____	233	accept positive peer pressure
_____	234	participate in group problem solving

•••

_____	135	participate in difficult games
_____	136	spontaneously participate in group activity
_____	137	disapprove of offensive peer behavior
_____	138	verbally indicate preferences for group members
_____	139	physically or verbally support another student
_____	140	participate in group problem solving
_____	141	spontaneously demonstrate positive leadership
_____	142	spontaneously resist negative peer pressure
_____	Individual	_____

Current Performance Form

Student _____ Teacher/Case Manager_____ Date_____

Summary of: Baseline___ 6TH WK___ 12TH WK___ 18TH WK___ 24TH WK___ 30TH WK___ 36TH WK___

Termination_____ Other_____ Performance Level: 3___ 2___ 1___

Task: Engages in learning tasks and activities that are assigned by teachers

_____	301	attempt academic tasks
_____	302	accept assistance on academic tasks
_____	303	demonstrate short-term memory for directions
_____	304	agree to complete testing
_____	305	appropriately seek assistance from an adult
_____	306	minimally participate in group-focused classes
_____	307	respond appropriately to begin and complete tasks
_____	308	watch audiovisual presentations
_____	309	refrain from inappropriate behavior when correcting errors
_____	310	participate in physical education class
_____	311	complete daily reading/English assignment
_____	312	complete daily math assignment
_____	313	work independently for 10-20 minutes
_____	314	attempt to verbally answer questions when called on

•••

_____	215	accept assistance on group academic tasks
_____	216	share and take turns during group tasks
_____	217	volunteer appropriate answers in group
_____	218	participate in physical education team activities
_____	219	actively participate in mini-classes
_____	220	choose and participate in elective classes
_____	221	work independently for 20-30 minutes
_____	222	ignore routine distractions during seat work
_____	223	correct assignment when given directions
_____	224	select an activity to occupy oneself
_____	225	self-chart progress in reading and/or math
_____	226	complete all assignments

•••

_____	127	participate in simulated mainstream classes
_____	128	use time productively while waiting for assistance
_____	129	contribute to class discussions and activities
_____	130	participate in role playing mainstream situations
_____	131	complete all assignments when due
_____	132	work independently for 30-40 minutes
_____	133	take a test following verbal/written directions
_____	134	seek and work independently on tasks
_____	135	complete and turn in homework when due
_____	Individual	_____

Personal: Engages in dialog to resolve issues, develop skills, and build self-worth

_____	301	attend sessions under duress
_____	302	demonstrate attention by eye contact/restating
_____	303	participate verbally in session
_____	304	accept positive feedback from an adult
_____	305	express negative feelings to an adult
_____	306	verbally acknowledge and describe personal feelings
_____	307	accept feedback about feelings
_____	308	follow through with directions to modify behavior
_____	309	initiate verbal interaction by requesting counseling
_____	310	remain seated during counseling sessions
_____	311	listen to alternatives and choose one
_____	312	verbalize that he/she has friends
_____	313	verbalize understanding of logical consequences
_____	314	accurately recall events
_____	315	verbally initiate positive interactions with an adult
_____	316	remain on counseling task/topic
_____	317	participate in short-term planning
_____	318	negotiate and complete terms of daily contract
_____	319	react with appropriate emotional response
_____	320	verbalize feelings about self to an adult
_____	321	verbalize consequences for own behavior

•••

_____	222	verbally describe characteristics of friendships
_____	223	verbally acknowledge misdirected anger
_____	224	attend to a peer when peer is speaking
_____	225	appropriately accept positive feedback from peers
_____	226	provide peers with appropriate feedback
_____	227	accept leadership role in group
_____	228	express feelings about self to peer
_____	229	verbalize desire to return to less restrictive setting
_____	230	seek counseling to avoid conflict
_____	231	attend counseling without objections
_____	232	participate in compromise
_____	233	participate in personal plan for one to six weeks
_____	234	verbally describe distressful situations
_____	235	verbally demonstrate that stress is normal
_____	236	participate in short-term planning for the group
_____	237	verbally accept conforming to a decision

•••

_____	138	use behavior to express pride
_____	139	list consequences of own behavior
_____	140	contribute to making group rules and consequences
_____	141	participate in group plan for 2-5 weeks
_____	142	initiate goal setting for self
_____	143	initiate problem solving or compromise for self
_____	144	initiate problem solving or compromise for group
_____	145	verbalize understanding of regular school
_____	146	verbally demonstrate knowledge of coping strategies
_____	147	verbally support others for appropriate behaviors
_____	148	discuss the value of relationships
_____	149	initiate and maintain relationships
_____	Individual	_____

LEVEL 3 Baseline Recording Form

Student _____   Observer _____   Begin Date _____   End Date _____

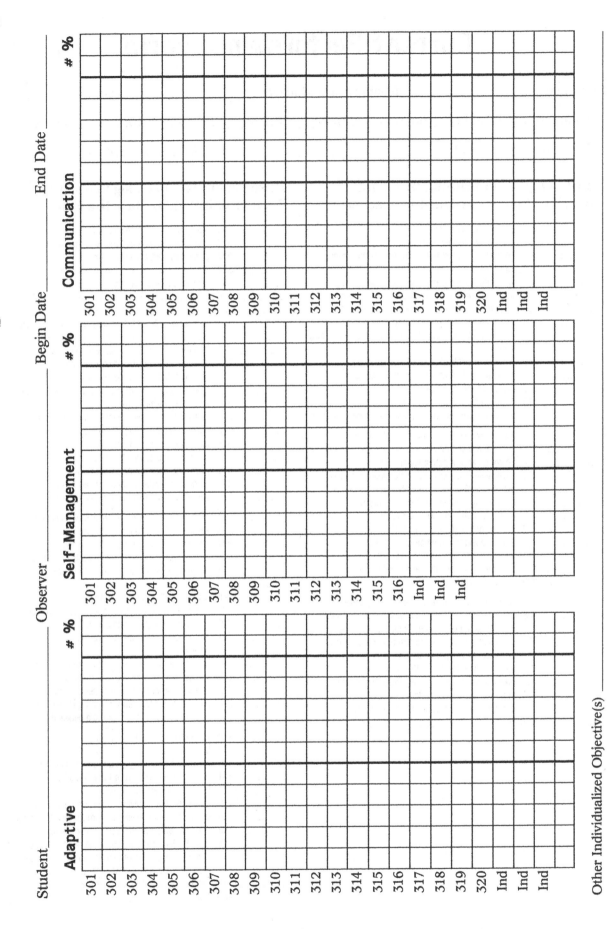

Adaptive # %

301
302
303
304
305
306
307
308
309
310
311
312
313
314
315
316
317
318
319
320
Ind
Ind
Ind

Self-Management # %

301
302
303
304
305
306
307
308
309
310
311
312
313
314
315
316
Ind
Ind
Ind

Communication # %

301
302
303
304
305
306
307
308
309
310
311
312
313
314
315
316
317
318
319
320
Ind
Ind
Ind

Other Individualized Objective(s) _____

Mark boxes: X = Demonstrated   O = Not Demonstrated   N = Not Observed   A = Absent   # = Number of Days Demonstrated   % = # ÷ 10

BOS

LEVEL 3 Baseline Recording Form

Student _____ Observer _____ Begin Date _____ End Date _____

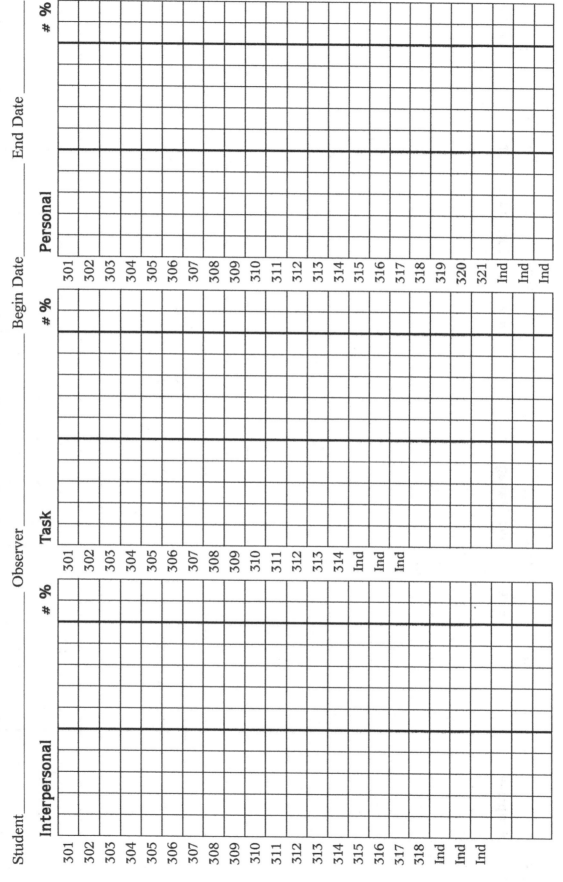

Interpersonal | # % | **Task** | # % | **Personal** | # %

301, 302, 303, 304, 305, 306, 307, 308, 309, 310, 311, 312, 313, 314, 315, 316, 317, 318, Ind, Ind, Ind

301, 302, 303, 304, 305, 306, 307, 308, 309, 310, 311, 312, 313, 314, Ind, Ind, Ind

301, 302, 303, 304, 305, 306, 307, 308, 309, 310, 311, 312, 313, 314, 315, 316, 317, 318, 319, 320, 321, Ind, Ind, Ind

Other Individualized Objective(s) _____

Mark boxes: X = Demonstrated   O = Not Demonstrated   N = Not Observed   A = Absent   # = Number of Days Demonstrated   % = # ÷ 10

LEVEL 2 Baseline Recording Form

Student _____   Observer _____   Begin Date _____   End Date _____

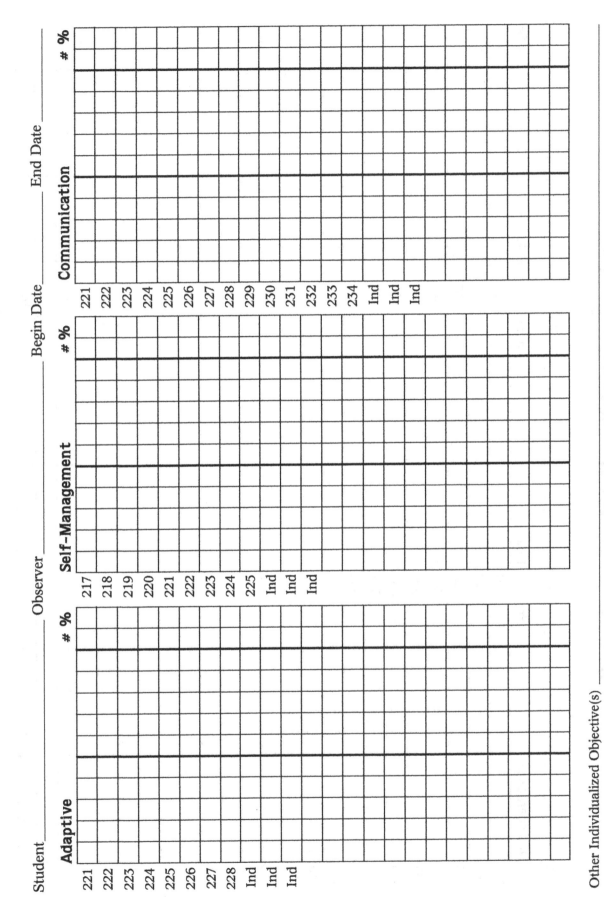

Adaptive

%

221
222
223
224
225
226
227
228
Ind
Ind
Ind

Self-Management

%

217
218
219
220
221
222
223
224
225
Ind
Ind
Ind

Communication

%

221
222
223
224
225
226
227
228
229
230
231
232
233
234
Ind
Ind
Ind

Other Individualized Objective(s) _____

Mark boxes: X = Demonstrated   O = Not Demonstrated   N = Not Observed   A = Absent   # = Number of Days Demonstrated   % = # ÷ 10

BOS

LEVEL 2 Baseline Recording Form

Student _____   Observer _____   Begin Date _____   End Date _____

BOS

Interpersonal

	#	%
219		
220		
221		
222		
223		
224		
225		
226		
227		
228		
229		
230		
231		
232		
233		
234		
Ind		
Ind		
Ind		

Task

	#	%
215		
216		
217		
218		
219		
220		
221		
222		
223		
224		
225		
226		
Ind		
Ind		
Ind		

Personal

	#	%
222		
223		
224		
225		
226		
227		
228		
229		
230		
231		
232		
233		
234		
235		
236		
237		
Ind		
Ind		
Ind		

Other Individualized Objective(s) _____

Mark boxes: X = Demonstrated   O = Not Demonstrated   N = Not Observed   A = Absent   # = Number of Days Demonstrated   % = # ÷ 10

Behavioral Objective Sequence

LEVEL 1 Baseline Recording Form

Student _____   Observer _____   Begin Date _____   End Date _____

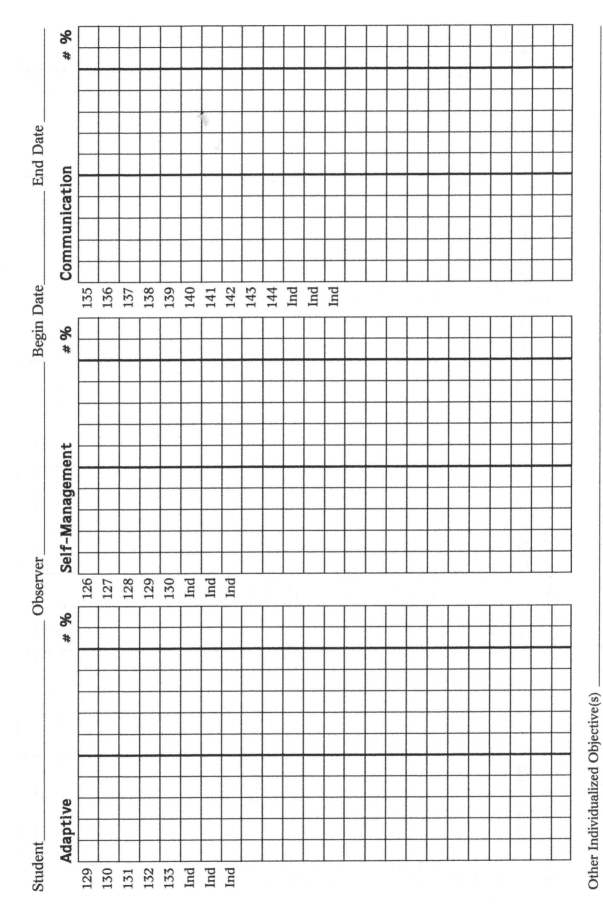

Adaptive

129
130
131
132
133
Ind
Ind
Ind

Self-Management

126
127
128
129
130
Ind
Ind
Ind

Communication

135
136
137
138
139
140
141
142
143
144
Ind
Ind
Ind

%   # %   # %

Other Individualized Objective(s) _____

Mark boxes: X = Demonstrated   O = Not Demonstrated   N = Not Observed   A = Absent   # = Number of Days Demonstrated   % = # ÷ 10

BOS

LEVEL 1 Baseline Recording Form

Student _____ Observer _____ Begin Date _____ End Date _____

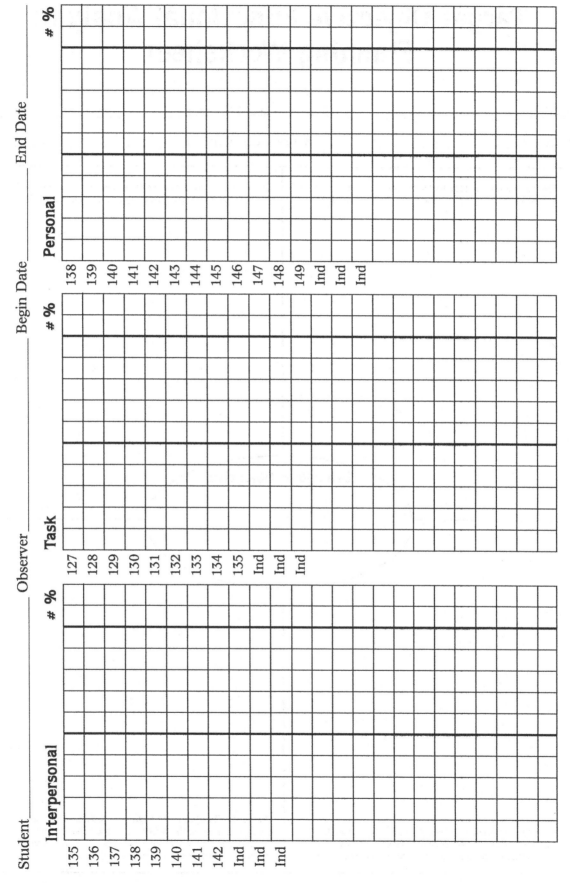

Interpersonal	#	%
135		
136		
137		
138		
139		
140		
141		
142		
Ind		
Ind		
Ind		

Task	#	%
127		
128		
129		
130		
131		
132		
133		
134		
135		
Ind		
Ind		
Ind		

Personal	#	%
138		
139		
140		
141		
142		
143		
144		
145		
146		
147		
148		
149		
Ind		
Ind		
Ind		

Other Individualized Objective(s) _____

Mark boxes: X = Demonstrated   O = Not Demonstrated   N = Not Observed   A = Absent   # = Number of Days Demonstrated   % = # ÷ 10

Target Objective Functional Analysis Planning Worksheet

Student _____ Teacher/Case Manager _____

Date _____ Worksheet Number _____

Environmental Antecedents: Describe environmental events that typically precede or appear to elicit the behavior.

Environmental Consequences: Describe environmental events that typically follow or appear to reinforce/inhibit the behavior.

Behavioral Objective

Personal Antecedents: Describe health, background, relationships, and measures of achievement, interests, and motivation that may have general effects on the behavior.

Personal Thoughts and Feelings: Describe what the student says about the "meaning" of the behavior and its consequences as well as inferences about thoughts and feelings derived from observations of the student.

Functional Analysis
Planning Worksheet Summary

Student _____ Teacher/Case Manager _____

School/Agency _____ Date _____

Team Members _____

I. Assessment

Problem Description

Target behavior(s) _____

Environmental antecedents (Who, What, Where, When) _____

_____

Environmental consequences _____

Personal consequences_____

Student strengths and weaknesses_____

_____

Possible contributing factors _____

Procedures already tried and evaluations of their success _____

_____

A positive vision for the student's performance _____

II. The Plan

Objective #1 _____ Priority _____

Intervention (What) _____

Implementation (Who, Where, When, How) _____

Progress evaluation (Who, When, What)_____

Objective #2 _____ Priority _____

Intervention (What) _____

Implementation (Who, Where, When, How) _____

Progress evaluation (Who, When, What)_____

Objective #3 _____ Priority _____

Intervention (What) _____

Implementation (Who, Where, When, How) _____

Progress evaluation (Who, When, What)_____

III. Follow-up

Person responsible for _____ by date _____

Person responsible for _____ by date _____

Results:

Repeat steps if necessary.

Behavioral Objective Sequence

Individual Intervention Plan Form

BOS

School/Agency _____

Student _____ ID# _____ Teacher/Case Manager _____ Performance Level _____

Begin Date _____ End Date _____ Number of Days/Weeks _____ Plan No. _____

Objectives	Plan (Be specific)	PP	FCD	FCE	TS	LOG
Adaptive # # #						
Self-Management # # #						
Communication # # #						
Interpersonal # # #						
Task # # #						

Behavioral Objective Sequence

BOS

Objectives	Plan (Be specific)	PP	FCD	FCE	TS	LOG
Personal # # #						
Other Objectives # # #						
Family Contact Progress Reporting Conference Other	_____ will call/write to report progress and/or problems at least _____ time(s). _____ will send progress report every _____ weeks. _____ will invite parent/guardian to conference for the purpose of:					
Regular School Contact Person(s)	_____ will send progress report every _____ weeks. _____ will arrange conference for the purpose of:					
Agency Person(s)	_____ will call/write to report progress and/or problems at least _____ time(s). _____ will arrange conference for the purpose of:					

Additional Service Provided:

☐ Adaptive PE _____ Min. per week   ☐ LD Resource _____ Min. per week   ☐ Speech/Lang. _____ Min. per week
☐ Psychologist _____ Min. per week   ☐ OT/PT _____ Min. per week   ☐ Drug Coun. _____ Min. per week
☐ Nurse _____ Min. per week   ☐ Medication(s) _____   ☐ Restrictions _____

PP = Permanent Product   FCD = Frequency Count by Day   FCE = Frequency Count by Event   TS = Time Sample   Log = Narrative

Daily Monitoring Record

Student _____ ID# _____ Teacher/Case Manager _____

Begin Date _____ End Date _____ Number of Days Present _____ Days Absent _____ % Present _____

Objective # Description	1st Week	2nd Week	3rd Week	4th Week	5th Week	6th Week	%
Adaptive							
Self-Management							
Communi-cation							
Interpersonal							
Task							
Personal							

Key: X = Student DID meet performance criteria for the day.   O = Student did NOT meet performance criteria for the day.

BOS

Team Meeting Notes

Student_____ Team Leader _____

Date

_____

School-Community Agency Coordinated Intervention Plan

Student _____ School _____

Teacher _____ Support Staff _____

Agency _____ Staff _____

_____   _____

Begin Date _____ Review Date _____ End Date _____

Specific Plans (Who will do What? When? Where?)

Student Goals/ Objectives	School Plan	Agency Plan	Monitoring Plan

Behavioral Objective Sequence

Copyright © 1998 by Sheldon Braaten

Interagency Meeting Notes

Student_____ Team Leader_____

Date	Participants	Agency

Target Behavior Performance Chart

Begin Date _____

End Date _____

Chart Number _____

of _____

Student _____ Teacher/Case Manager _____ School/Agency _____

Behavioral Objective(s) or Description _____

$\overline{X}$

%

																		Summary

Frequency/Level of Performance

20 19 18 17 16 15 14 13 12 11 10 9 8 7 6 5 4 3 2 1

1 2 3 4 5 6 7 8 9 10 11 12 13 14 15 16 17 18 19 20 21 22 23 24 25 26 27 28 29 30 31 32 33 34 35

Baseline   Intervention Plan

Trials – Opportunities – Days

Target Behavior Performance Chart

Begin Date _____

End Date _____

Student _____ Teacher/Case Manager _____ School/Agency _____

Behavioral Objective(s) or Description _____

Chart Number _____ of _____

$\overline{X}$ %

100																																					
95																																					
90																																					
85																																					
80																																					
75																																					
70																																					
65																																					
60																																					
55																																					
50																																					
45																																					
40																																					
35																																					
30																																					
25																																					
20																																					
15																																					
10																																					
5																																					

Frequency/Level of Performance

1 2 3 4 5 6 7 8 9 10 11 12 13 14 15 16 17 18 19 20 21 22 23 24 25 26 27 28 29 30 31 32 33 34 35 Summary

Baseline Intervention Plan

Trials – Opportunities – Days

Target Behavior Performance Chart

Begin Date _____

End Date _____

Student _____ Teacher/Case Manager _____

School/Agency _____

Behavioral Objective(s) or Description _____

Chart Number _____ of _____

$\overline{X}$ %

Frequency/Level of Performance

0 1 2 3 4 5 6 7 8 9 10 11 12 13 14 15 16 17 18 19 20 21 22 23 24 25 26 27 28 29 30 31 32 33 34 35   Summary

Baseline   Intervention Plan

Trials – Opportunities – Days

Target Behavior Performance Chart

Begin Date _____   Chart Number _____

End Date _____   _____ of _____

Student _____   Teacher/Case Manager _____   School/Agency _____

Behavioral Objective(s) or Description _____

X̄																																					%

Percent/Level of Performance

% : 100 95 90 85 80 75 70 65 60 55 50 45 40 35 30 25 20 15 10 5

1 2 3 4 5 6 7 8 9 10 11 12 13 14 15 16 17 18 19 20 21 22 23 24 25 26 27 28 29 30 31 32 33 34 35 Summary

Baseline   Intervention Plan

Trials – Opportunities – Days

Behavioral Progress Report

Student _____ Date from _____ to _____

Teacher/Case Manager _____ School/Agency _____

Attendance: Days Present _____ Days Absent _____ Days Tardy _____

Performance Guide: 1 = consistently 2 = frequently 3 = sometimes 4 = rarely 5 = never

Current Behavioral Objectives	Performance	Comments

Academic Objectives

Other Notes

Signed _____ Date _____

Annual Progress Summary Form

Student _____ School Year/Term_____

Student I.D. Number_____ School/Program_____

Record the target objectives' numbers from the BOS subscales at the beginning of each monitoring interval. At the end of the interval, record whether the student mastered the objective during the interval by circling "Y" for Yes or "N" for No. For 6-week monitoring plans, use each column. For intervals of a different duration (e.g., 12-week, 18-week, 6-month), indicate the duration for the period being recorded.

Progress monitoring summary interval: ___6-week ___12-week ___18-week ___6-month

Duration	First _____	Second _____	Third _____	Fourth _____	Fifth _____	Sixth _____
Adaptive	#____ Y N	#____ Y N	#____ Y N	#____ Y N	#____ Y N	#____ Y N
	#____ Y N	#____ Y N	#____ Y N	#____ Y N	#____ Y N	#____ Y N
	#____ Y N	#____ Y N	#____ Y N	#____ Y N	#____ Y N	#____ Y N
	#____ Y N	#____ Y N	#____ Y N	#____ Y N	#____ Y N	#____ Y N
Self-Management	#____ Y N	#____ Y N	#____ Y N	#____ Y N	#____ Y N	#____ Y N
	#____ Y N	#____ Y N	#____ Y N	#____ Y N	#____ Y N	#____ Y N
	#____ Y N	#____ Y N	#____ Y N	#____ Y N	#____ Y N	#____ Y N
	#____ Y N	#____ Y N	#____ Y N	#____ Y N	#____ Y N	#____ Y N
Communication	#____ Y N	#____ Y N	#____ Y N	#____ Y N	#____ Y N	#____ Y N
	#____ Y N	#____ Y N	#____ Y N	#____ Y N	#____ Y N	#____ Y N
	#____ Y N	#____ Y N	#____ Y N	#____ Y N	#____ Y N	#____ Y N
	#____ Y N	#____ Y N	#____ Y N	#____ Y N	#____ Y N	#____ Y N
Interpersonal	#____ Y N	#____ Y N	#____ Y N	#____ Y N	#____ Y N	#____ Y N
	#____ Y N	#____ Y N	#____ Y N	#____ Y N	#____ Y N	#____ Y N
	#____ Y N	#____ Y N	#____ Y N	#____ Y N	#____ Y N	#____ Y N
	#____ Y N	#____ Y N	#____ Y N	#____ Y N	#____ Y N	#____ Y N
Task	#____ Y N	#____ Y N	#____ Y N	#____ Y N	#____ Y N	#____ Y N
	#____ Y N	#____ Y N	#____ Y N	#____ Y N	#____ Y N	#____ Y N
	#____ Y N	#____ Y N	#____ Y N	#____ Y N	#____ Y N	#____ Y N
	#____ Y N	#____ Y N	#____ Y N	#____ Y N	#____ Y N	#____ Y N
Personal	#____ Y N	#____ Y N	#____ Y N	#____ Y N	#____ Y N	#____ Y N
	#____ Y N	#____ Y N	#____ Y N	#____ Y N	#____ Y N	#____ Y N
	#____ Y N	#____ Y N	#____ Y N	#____ Y N	#____ Y N	#____ Y N
	#____ Y N	#____ Y N	#____ Y N	#____ Y N	#____ Y N	#____ Y N
Non-BOS Objectives	#____ Y N	#____ Y N	#____ Y N	#____ Y N	#____ Y N	#____ Y N
	#____ Y N	#____ Y N	#____ Y N	#____ Y N	#____ Y N	#____ Y N
	#____ Y N	#____ Y N	#____ Y N	#____ Y N	#____ Y N	#____ Y N
Completor's Initials	_____	_____	_____	_____	_____	_____

Behavioral Objective Sequence